CONQUERING THROUGH CONFLICT

A STUDY OF 2 PETER

BIBLE STUDY GUIDE

From the Bible-teaching ministry of

Charles R. Swindoll

INSIGHT FOR LIVING

Charles R. Swindoll is a graduate of Dallas Theological Seminary and has served in pastorates in Texas, Massachusetts, and California since 1963. He has served as senior pastor of the First Evangelical Free Church of Fullerton, California, since 1971. Chuck's radio program, "Insight for Living," began in 1979. In addition to his church and radio ministries, Chuck enjoys writing. He has authored numerous books and booklets on a variety of subjects.

Based on the outlines and transcripts of Chuck's sermons, the study guide text is co-authored by Lee Hough, a graduate of The University of Texas at Arlington and Dallas Theological Seminary.

Editor in Chief:
Cynthia Swindoll

Coauthor of Text:
Lee Hough

Assistant Editor:
Wendy Peterson

Copyediting Supervisor:
Marty Anderson

Copy Editor:
Marty Anderson

Designer:
Diana Vasquez

Production Artists:
Robert McGuire and Gary Lett

Typographer:
Bob Haskins

Director, Communications Division:
Carla Meberg

Project Manager:
Alene Cooper

Print Production Manager:
Deedee Snyder

Assistant Production Manager:
John Norton

Printer:
Frye and Smith

Unless otherwise identified, all Scripture references are from the New American Standard Bible, © The Lockman Foundation 1960, 1962, 1963, 1968, 1971, 1972, 1973, 1975, 1977. Used by permission.

Scripture quotations marked (NIV) are taken from the Holy Bible, New International Version. Copyright © 1973, 1978, 1984 International Bible Society. Used by permission of Zondervan Bible Publishers.

An effort has been made to locate sources and obtain permission where necessary for the quotations used in this book. In the event of any unintentional omission, a modification will gladly be incorporated in future printings.

ISBN 0-8499-8422-X

Printed in the United States of America.

COVER PAINTING: *The Transfiguration* by Carl Bloch. Used by permission of Frederiksborg Museum, Hillerod, Denmark. "In the third year of His ministry Jesus took Peter, James, and John to the top of Mount Tabor. There He was transfigured and Elijah and Moses appeared and talked with Him. From a cloud a voice said that this was His beloved son. *Mark 9:7.*" *The Holy Bible: Authorized King James Version, with full-color illustrations of the Old Masters* (Charlotte, N.C.: Bible House, 1960), caption for a copy of the painting.

CONTENTS

INTRODUCTION

Although not nearly as long as his first letter, Peter's second letter is much more difficult to understand and, for that matter, to "enjoy." In these three chapters, the apostle addresses, in depth, many of the characteristics of evil. With vivid terminology he describes both the life-style and the wicked influence of the ungodly. In some ways, 2 Peter will remind Bible students of the one-chapter letter of Jude.

But through it all, Peter is quick to remind us that the believer can and will conquer through conflict. Times may be harsh and corruption rampant, but those whose faith rests in the Lord will not only survive, they will be victorious.

I commend these studies to you. While the subjects may not be "bedside reading," the effort you invest will be well rewarded. After all, to be forewarned is to be forearmed.

Stand firm, my friend!

Chuck Swindoll

Chuck Swindoll

PUTTING TRUTH
INTO ACTION

K nowledge apart from application falls short of God's desire for His children. He wants us to apply what we learn so that we will change and grow. This study guide was prepared with these goals in mind. As you go through the following pages, we hope your desire to discover biblical truth will grow as your understanding of God's Word increases, and that you will be encouraged to apply what you've learned.

To assist you in your study, we've included a section called **Living Insights** at the end of each lesson. These exercises will challenge you to study further and to think of specific ways to put your discoveries into action.

There are many ways to use this guide—in personal devotions, group studies, discussions with friends and family, and Sunday school classes. And, of course, it's an ideal study aid when you're listening to its corresponding "Insight for Living" radio series.

To benefit most from this study guide, we would encourage you to consider it a spiritual journal. That's why we've included space in the **Living Insights** for recording your thoughts and discoveries. We hope you'll return to those sections often for review and encouragement as you continue to grow in your walk with Christ.

Lee Hough
Coauthor of Text

CONQUERING THROUGH CONFLICT

A STUDY OF 2 PETER

Chapter 1

A LETTER THAT RATTLES OUR CAGE

Survey of 2 Peter

Have you ever noticed how sequels are rarely as good as their originals?

Take movies, for example. Most of us can probably still feel the terror of *Jaws*—still see the image of that hideous great white shark erupting out of the water to devour unsuspecting swimmers in a bloody frenzy. But *Jaws II?* It barely causes a ripple in our memories. And who of us doesn't have imprinted on our souls Judy Garland and her friends dancing down that yellow brick road through a sparkling, Technicolored land in *The Wizard of Oz?* But *The Return to Oz?* Well, it didn't exactly take us over the rainbow, now did it?

This rule of disappointing sequels is usually true when it comes to movies, books, toys, and even cars. But the exception to this rule is the Bible. From 2 Samuel to 3 John, biblical sequels retain as much value and significance as their predecessors. And, as we will discover in today's lesson, the second letter from Peter's pen is just as inspired and inspiring as the first.

But before we dig into a verse-by-verse study, let's spend some time surveying this little book—sort of take in a preview of 2 Peter's coming attractions.

A Few Introductory Comments

Around A.D. 64 churches scattered throughout five Roman provinces in Asia Minor received a second letter from the apostle Peter. Save that of Jude's, this letter is perhaps the most intense epistle in the New Testament. Unlike his first letter, which offered hope to those experiencing persecution, Peter designed his second letter to rattle some cages. It did, and it still does. Let's make four brief introductory observations about this power-packed letter.

1

First: *Many people aren't aware that Peter's second letter is more difficult to read than his first.* We naively assume that since 2 Peter isn't very long, it shouldn't be hard to understand. So we plunge right in and immediately start to flounder. We lose our footing on slippery ambiguities, and we're swept away by the swift, strong currents of the book's theme. Fortunately, some readers have a good Bible commentary they can grab onto at this point. But most simply bail out of the book without ever finishing it.

However, not everything about 2 Peter is difficult to grasp. Both at the beginning and at the end of his letter Peter clearly states his purpose for writing.

> Therefore, I shall always be ready to remind you of these things, even though you already know them, and have been established in the truth which is present with you. And I consider it right, as long as I am in this earthly dwelling, to *stir you up* by way of reminder. (1:12–13, emphasis added)

> This is now, beloved, the second letter I am writing to you in which I am *stirring up* your sincere mind by way of reminder. (3:1, emphasis added)

The apostle wanted to stir them up, to rattle some cages in hopes that it would spur his readers on to be more diligent in the exercise of their faith.

> Therefore, brethren, be all the more diligent to make certain about His calling and choosing you; for as long as you practice these things, you will never stumble. . . .
> Therefore, beloved, since you look for these things, be diligent to be found by Him in peace, spotless and blameless. (1:10; 3:14)

Second: *The concern in this letter is different from that in the first.* First Peter focuses on external sources of hardship, such as unfair slave owners, a pagan society, and an increasingly unsympathetic emperor. Second Peter, on the other hand, is concerned with internal sources of corruption, namely, false prophets who are deceitfully gaining footholds in local assemblies.[1]

---

1. Second Peter and Jude share not only a similar intensity but also a similar concern (see Jude 3–4).

Third: *Second Peter is strange, surprising, and occasionally severe.* You will be surprised not only by Peter's topics and candor but also by what he deliberately omits in his letter. Traditional subjects, such as Christ's suffering, resurrection, and ascension; the Holy Spirit; prayer; and baptism, are never mentioned. And a passionate call for his readers to model Jesus' example is also noticeably absent.[2] Because of these pronounced omissions and the different style,[3] 2 Peter stirred up quite a debate over its canonicity.

> During the fourth century, the great church historian, Eusebius . . . listed 2 Peter, along with 2 and 3 John and James, as antilegomena, books whose canonicity was under dispute. . . .
>
> Jerome . . . included 2 Peter in his well-known translation of the Bible, the Latin Vulgate. Though Jerome accepted the authenticity of the book, he stated that many questioned its Petrine authorship because of the marked difference of style between 1 and 2 Peter.[4]

Finally, after prolonged scrutiny, the church council of Laodicea, in A.D. 366, officially recognized 2 Peter as belonging in the canon of Scripture.

Fourth: *The themes in Peter's second letter are more subtle and indirect than those in his first.* So much so that they're almost obscure! The most obvious theme is Peter's resolve to stir up diligence during difficult times. But upon closer inspection, we will find two other closely related themes.

Three Themes Woven through the Letter

The three themes of 2 Peter fit together like the feathers, shaft, and point of an arrow. The feathers are made up of *warnings:* "Watch

---

2. In contrast to what is omitted, 2 Peter includes something no other New Testament letter does. In verses 14–16 of chapter 3, Peter mentions another biblical writer—Paul, "our beloved brother."

3. Proportionately, 2 Peter has the highest number of words that appear only once in the New Testament, called *hapax legomena.* And of those fifty-four words, thirty-two are not even found in the Septuagint—the Greek version of the Old Testament.

4. Kenneth O. Gangel, "2 Peter," in *The Bible Knowledge Commentary,* New Testament ed., ed. John F. Walvoord and Roy B. Zuck (Wheaton, Ill.: SP Publications, Victor Books, 1983), p. 859.

out, beware"; *reminders:* "Remember, don't forget"; and *promises:* "It will come to pass, count on this." These feathers, however, amount to nothing more than spiritual-sounding fluff if we don't act on them. So label the main shaft *diligence.* Peter will tell us more than once that if diligence is applied it will lead to the arrow's point—*hope!*

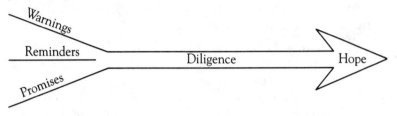

A Brief Overview

Second Peter is a short book with only sixty-one verses spread out over three chapters. But, as we noted earlier, this letter is not easily navigated. So on the facing page is a brief chart to give you an idea of where we'll be heading and what we can expect.

The first three verses of chapter 1 are introductory. Peter tells us who he is—"a bond-servant and apostle of Jesus Christ"—and that he wrote the letter. In the balance of chapter 1 Peter addresses the moral corruption of the last days. He focuses on answering the pressing question "How can we avoid being corrupted?" To this, Peter gives three answers. He issues a *warning* to stay pure (v. 4), he stirs us up by way of *reminder* (vv. 12–13), and he holds out a *promise* (v. 10).

Chapter 2 shifts from moral corruption to the second major issue of the last days, doctrinal compromise. Here, in verses 1–3a, Peter answers the question "What shall I expect from so-called prophets?" with a warning.

> There will also be false teachers among you, who will secretly introduce destructive heresies, even denying the Master who bought them, bringing swift destruction upon themselves. And many will follow their sensuality, and because of them the way of the truth will be maligned; and in their greed they will exploit you with false words.

The false prophets of Peter's day and of our own all share four basic traits. First, they're more interested in gaining popularity than

4

SURVEY OF 2 PETER

Purpose: To warn against false teaching, moral compromise, and doctrinal error in the last days.

Date: A.D. 66–67

Key Words: Know, Diligence, Remember / Remind, Corruption

Tone: Urgency, Intensity

	Moral Corruption	Doctrinal Compromise	Prophetic Concern	Conclusion
Introduction	*Answers Question:*	*Answers Question:*	*Answers Question:*	
	How can I escape defilement?	What shall I expect from "prophets"?	Where will all this end?	
1:1–3	Chapter 1	Chapter 2	Chapter 3	3:18
Warning	Be Pure! (v. 4)	Be Aware! (vv. 1–3)	Be Strong! (v. 14)	
Reminder	Verses 12–13	Verses 21–22	Verses 1–2	
Promise	"You will never stumble" (v. 10)	"God will rescue you" (v. 9)	"We look for new hope" (v. 13)	
Perspective	Looking within	Looking back	Looking ahead	

in declaring truth. Second, they're more interested in receiving than in giving—whether it's money, fame, or power. Third, their personal lives model a seduction toward evil. And fourth, they ultimately lead people from God, not to Him.

But though these religious pied pipers will lead many to destruction, not everyone will be captivated by their lies. Peter offers hope for escaping their deluding influence with this promise: "The Lord knows how to rescue the godly from temptation" (v. 9a).

Crossing over into chapter three, Peter focuses his attention on prophetic concerns. The subject of future things will always bring those who want to indoctrinate us with their twisted brand of teaching, using the latest fads to make their delusions more exciting and appealing. But Peter's advice is to stick with the orthodox teachings passed on by the apostles from the Lord Jesus (see 3:1–2).

Peter then goes on to cite a particular concern about the future.

> Know this first of all, that in the last days mockers will come with their mocking, following after their own lusts, and saying, "Where is the promise of His coming? For ever since the fathers fell asleep, all continues just as it was from the beginning of creation." (3:3–4)

These last-day mockers, known as uniformitarians,[5] scoff at the idea of a transcendent God who intervenes in human affairs. "The world has always plodded along according to its own natural processes," they say. Peter counters their shortsighted skepticism, however, with a brief history lesson from Genesis.

> For when they maintain this, it escapes their notice that by the word of God the heavens existed long ago and the earth was formed out of water and by water, through which the world at that time was destroyed, being flooded with water. (vv. 5–6)

They forget that there was a universal flood which interrupted everything! And if God could interrupt the world then, He can certainly do it again through His second coming. Moving on from the watery reminder of God's transcendency, Peter next pictures

---

5. *Uniformitarianism* is "a geological doctrine that existing processes acting in the same manner as at present are sufficient to account for all geological changes." *Webster's Ninth New Collegiate Dictionary*, see "uniformitarianism."

God as standing alone. He points out that *the Lord has a unique timetable.*

> But do not let this one fact escape your notice, beloved, that with the Lord one day is as a thousand years, and a thousand years as one day. (v. 8)

He has a different strategy.

> The Lord is not slow about His promise, as some count slowness, but is patient toward you, not wishing for any to perish but for all to come to repentance. (v. 9)

And *He has an unusual plan.*

> But the day of the Lord will come like a thief, in which the heavens will pass away with a roar and the elements will be destroyed with intense heat, and the earth and its works will be burned up. (v. 10)

Reflecting on these truths, Peter reminds us to live godly lives that testify to a future hope.

> Since all these things are to be destroyed in this way, what sort of people ought you to be in holy conduct and godliness, looking for and hastening the coming of the day of God, on account of which the heavens will be destroyed by burning, and the elements will melt with intense heat! But according to His promise we are looking for new heavens and a new earth, in which righteousness dwells. (vv. 11–13)

Then, in the remaining four verses, Peter closes with a final resounding plea for diligence (vv. 14–18).

Some Tips on Living a More Alert Life

Warren Wiersbe writes,

> If anybody in the early church knew the importance of being alert, it was the Apostle Peter. He had a tendency in his early years to feel overconfident when danger was near and to overlook the Master's warnings. He rushed ahead when he should have waited; he slept when he should have prayed; he talked when

he should have listened. He was a courageous, but careless, Christian.[6]

That was Peter in his early years. But as he matured, the apostle learned how to be alert, and his letter will teach us how too. Using each of the letters in the word *hope*, here are four important tips from our lesson for cultivating an alert spirit.

Heed what you already know (1:12–13; 3:1–2). Many of us already know enough truth to keep us strong no matter how tough times may get. So don't fall into the trap of simply storing up knowledge; practice it too!

Open your eyes and ears (2:1–3; 3:17). Discernment is not so much a gift as it is a developed skill. Pay attention to what is *not* being said as much as what is. Just because people use all the right words and look the part doesn't guarantee that they are speaking the truth; don't confuse charisma with orthodoxy. Instead, get in the habit of comparing what you hear with the Scriptures, just like the Bereans did in Acts 17:10–11. Learn to study people's lives as well as their words. And if the two don't match, be careful.

Pursue a godly lifestyle (3:11, 14). Almost without exception, whenever Christ's return or the end times are mentioned in the New Testament, the emphasis is on living a pure life.

Expect Christ's return (3:12). Does the way you live reflect the hope of Christ's return? If not, try this experiment to see how expecting Christ at any time can radically change the way you live. First thing tomorrow morning, pray through your day with the thought that Christ could return at any moment. Then periodically stop and remind yourself of this truth. You'll be surprised at how this can transform your perspective and encourage righteous living.

🍇 Living Insights   STUDY ONE

To acquaint yourself with 2 Peter, read over the letter in a paraphrased version such as *The Living Bible*. Then jot down your first impressions in relation to the following questions.

How would you describe the tone of the letter?

_____

_____

---

6. Warren W. Wiersbe, *Be Alert* (Wheaton, Ill.: SP Publications, Victor Books, 1984), p. 9.

If you compare the letter to a song, what would be some of the major chords or themes?

_____

_____

_____

_____

_____

What would be some of the minor ones?

_____

_____

_____

Do you see any similarities between 2 Peter and 1 Peter?

_____

_____

_____

Any distinct differences?

_____

_____

_____

In a paragraph, summarize the content of 2 Peter.

_____

_____

_____

_____

Now that you've gotten a grasp of 2 Peter's central message, let's move from a distant point of observation to an up-close-and-personal point of application.

What general feelings surfaced when you read the letter?

_____

_____

_____

Was there a specific verse that pierced your heart with its haunting message? Why did it affect you that way?

_____

_____

_____

_____

What was your favorite verse in 2 Peter? Write it down.

_____

_____

_____

Now, on a separate piece of paper, do something creative with this verse. Use it as the basis for a poem or a song. Or write a contemporary paraphrase of it. Or turn it into a prayer. Use your imagination and write from your heart.

Chapter 2

TO BE USEFUL AND FRUITFUL, HERE'S HOW

2 Peter 1:1–11

What does it take to sustain life? Food, air, water—certainly these meet our physical needs. But we need more than just these to live, because on a different plane exist gnawing hunger pangs for purpose and meaning. When these needs go unfulfilled, we wither and die inside.

Perhaps that's why a lingering illness is so hard to bear. We feel so useless just lying there while others feed and clothe us. Our body atrophies and, with it, sometimes our spirit.

These same feelings are what make being in prison so difficult, especially for those who become Christians there. Though forgiven by God, they still face years of living a seemingly unproductive life behind bars.

The elderly are no exception to these feelings either. Many feel like prisoners inside their own bodies; their minds still function, but their bodies don't. They become depressed, nagged by thoughts of uselessness. Especially when they remember the times they were in demand, when their opinions counted and their gifts were used.

Goethe once said, "A useless life is only an early death."[1] But the dread of such a death isn't limited to the sick, the prisoners, or the aged. Just ask the healthy, young person who is bored at work or has no work. Just ask the executive who stays busy to ward off the frustration of an empty personal life. Or ask Simon Peter.

When the cock punctuated his third denial of Jesus, Peter felt completely useless and afraid. What kind of disciple would boast about laying his life down for his Lord, and then deny Him three times that same night? *"Even though all may fall away, yet I will not."* That very night, however, the echo of those words cracked like a whip over his broken heart to drive him through the streets, weeping. A rock? Hardly. Peter felt as if his life had been shattered into

---

1. *The International Dictionary of Thoughts*, comp. John P. Bradley, Leo F. Daniels, Thomas C. Jones (Chicago, Ill.: J. G. Ferguson Publishing Co., 1969), p. 443.

a hundred useless pieces. But he didn't stay there. Years later he wrote a letter which detailed the steps that can bring us up from the early grave of a useless life to a full and fruitful life in Christ.

Introductory Remarks from Peter

Peter opens his letter by identifying its author, its recipients, and the faith that links the two together. He introduces himself (2 Pet. 1:1a) as the writer: "Simon Peter, a bond-servant and apostle of Jesus Christ." Even though he possesses the authority of an apostle, he describes himself first as Christ's servant.

Next, Peter names the letter's recipients: "those who have received a faith of the same kind as ours" (v. 1b). "Ours" refers to all Jews who, like Peter, believed in the Lord Jesus. But who are the "those" he's talking about?

> There can really be only one answer to that. They must once have been Gentiles in contradistinction to the Jews who were uniquely the chosen people of God. . . .
>
> Peter puts this very vividly, using a word which would at once strike an answering chord in the minds of those who heard it. Their faith is *equal in honour and privilege.* The Greek is *isotimos.* . . . This word was particularly used in connection with strangers and foreigners who were given equal citizenship in a city with the natives. . . .
>
> So Peter addresses his letter to those who had once been despised Gentiles but who had been given equal rights of citizenship with the Jews and even with the apostles themselves in the kingdom of God.[2]

The barriers separating Jew and Gentile have been removed "by the righteousness of our God and Savior, Jesus Christ" (v. 1c), making us all one in Christ (see also Eph. 2:11–22; 3:1–6).

After this, Peter blesses his readers.

> Grace and peace be multiplied to you in the knowledge of God and of Jesus our Lord. (v. 2)

---

2. William Barclay, *The Letters of James and Peter,* rev. ed., The Daily Bible Study Series (Philadelphia, Pa.: Westminster Press, 1976), p. 291.

The term used here for *knowledge* isn't referring simply to academic scholarship. It signifies a knowledge that comes only from intimate fellowship with the Lord. Because the more we can comprehend the meaning of who Jesus Christ is, the more we can understand the meaning of grace and the experience of peace.

Peter continues his thought from verse two as he writes,

> Seeing that His divine power has granted to us everything pertaining to life and godliness, through the true knowledge of Him who called us by His own glory and excellence. (v. 3)

When our daily lives are infused with God's divine power,[3] two things are accomplished. First, our relationships with others become more useful and fruitful. And, second, our relationship with the Lord increases in godliness.

All Christians are equipped with the power of God when they first believe. But simply possessing that power doesn't guarantee a useful and godly life. We must also *act* upon it.

God's Promises—Our Participation

In verses 4 through 9 we come to the flip side of God's grace— our diligence. But first Peter reminds us of God's promises.

What God Gives . . . and Why

> For by these He has granted to us His precious and magnificent promises, in order that by them you might become partakers of the divine nature, having escaped the corruption that is in the world by lust. (v. 4)

Someone once counted the number of promises made by God to mankind in the Bible and came up with a total of 7,487![4] Though not every promise applies to us today, there are still hundreds, even thousands that do. Promises such as eternal life for the believer (John 3:16), strength for the weary (Isa. 40:28–31), rewards for the obedient (Rev. 22:12), comfort for the struggling (2 Cor. 1:3–5),

---

3. The term Peter uses for *power* means "that which overcomes resistance."

4. Herbert Lockyer, *All the Promises of the Bible* (Grand Rapids, Mich.: Zondervan Publishing House, 1962), p. 10.

and hope for the dying (1 Cor. 15:53–57). Through these promises, Peter says, we become partakers of the divine nature, a nature that will enable us to escape the corruption of a world driven by lust.

What We Give God . . . and How

Now that he has told us of the power and promises God has provided for our growth, Peter next focuses on what we must supply to achieve the goal of a godly life.

> Now for this very reason also, applying all diligence, in your faith supply moral excellence, and in your moral excellence, knowledge; and in your knowledge, self-control, and in your self-control, perseverance, and in your perseverance, godliness; and in your godliness, brotherly kindness, and in your brotherly kindness, love. (vv. 5–7)

Before we look at each of the virtues Peter lists, let's briefly examine how they find a place in our lives. The Greek term for *diligence* used here means "to make haste, to be eager." God equips us with power, but for our part we must apply diligence. Diligence serves as a catalyst that releases God's power and brings about change. It transforms theory into reality. Now let's study Peter's list of character traits that are worth our diligent effort.

Faith: Faith is the foundation of the Christian life; it's the firm conviction that God's Word is true. In practical terms, it means abandoning ourselves to His will, His strength, and His wisdom.

Moral excellence: At the root of this term is the idea of courage—in classical Greek it was used to indicate bravery and valor. So by using this word, Peter is encouraging us to strengthen our faith with the courage to stand firm in the truth, unswayed by majority opinion.

Knowledge: The Greek term *gnōsis*, meaning practical knowledge, is one of Peter's favorite words. It refers to a commonsense approach to applying biblical principles in our daily circumstances.

Self-control: Literally, this word means, "the ability to take a grip of oneself."[5] Nothing is to master us but the Master Himself. Not work, sex, food, or any of the other things that can so easily control our lives. Self-control means that, with God's help, we can live a more balanced life—even in a world where overindulgence is hyped as the highway to happiness.

---

5. Barclay, *Letters of James and Peter,* p. 302.

Perseverance: Chrysostom called this "The Queen of the Virtues."[6] The Greek word for *perseverance* is often translated "patience."

> But *patience* is too passive a word. . . . Cicero defines *patientia*, its Latin equivalent, as: "The voluntary and daily suffering of hard and difficult things, for the sake of honour and usefulness."[7]

Godliness: This refers to an authentic piety that's directed in two ways. First, there's a right attitude toward God, reflected in worship and obedience. Second, there's a right attitude toward others, evidenced by showing respect and a servant's heart.

Brotherly kindness: The brotherly kindness that Christ intends for us to display involves bearing one another's burdens (see Gal. 6:2). We're to come out of our ivory theological towers and get involved in helping others in the trenches of life. We need to make room for other people's opinions, feelings, and suggestions. And we've got to be willing to see life through their eyes.

Christian love: The top rung of Peter's eight-step ladder is love. It's the one virtue that comprises and unites all the others. The term used is *agapē*, which is best defined as "seeking the highest good of the other person." And that includes loving the unlovely, just as God in Christ has done for us (see Rom. 5:8).

What a list! It's no wonder Peter prefaces it with the assurance of divine power and the need for diligence. Both will be needed in abundance if we're to see these qualities come to fruition in our lives.

Finally, Peter tells us the purpose behind cultivating all these virtues.

> For if these qualities are yours and are increasing, they render you neither useless nor unfruitful in the true knowledge of our Lord Jesus Christ. (v. 8)

Developing a fruitful life in Christ is a process. There will always be bad habits to prune, improper thoughts to weed, and pure motives to water. To the diligent, God promises the rich harvest of a useful and godly life. But Peter says that the person who neglects sowing these traits

> is blind or shortsighted, having forgotten his purification from his former sins. (v. 9)

---

6. Quoted by Barclay in *Letters of James and Peter,* p. 303.
7. Quoted by Barclay in *Letters of James and Peter,* p. 303. See also Hebrews 12:2.

Commentator Michael Green illuminates the meaning of this verse for us.

> If a man is blind, how can he be short-sighted? If Peter had this meaning in mind, he may mean that such a man is blind to heavenly things, and engrossed in the earthly; he cannot see what is afar off, but only what is near. . . . But probably Peter was thinking . . . that such a man is blind because he blinks or willfully closes his eyes to the light. Spiritual blindness descends upon the eyes which deliberately look away from the graces of character to which the Christian is called when he comes to know Christ.[8]

The summit of Peter's opening paragraph is finally reached in verses 10–11.

> Therefore, brethren, be all the more diligent to make certain about His calling and choosing you; for as long as you practice these things, you will never stumble; for in this way the entrance into the eternal kingdom of our Lord and Savior Jesus Christ will be abundantly supplied to you.

But what does Peter mean by "be all the more diligent to make certain . . ."?

Where It All Leads . . . and When

These verses aren't telling us that unless we make a supreme effort we'll not be saved. Rather, they're a passionate appeal to live out the truth of our having been called and chosen. Kenneth Gangel writes,

> One's godly behavior is a warranty deed for himself that Jesus Christ has cleansed him from his past sins and therefore that he was in fact called and elected by God.[9]

8. Michael Green, *The Second Epistle General of Peter and the General Epistle of Jude* (Grand Rapids, Mich.: William B. Eerdmans Publishing Co., 1968), pp. 72–73. The Greek term for short-sighted is *myopazon*, from which we get the English word *myopia*. Webster defines *myopia* as "a lack of foresight or discernment" (*Webster's Ninth New Collegiate Dictionary*, see "myopia").

9. Kenneth O. Gangel, "2 Peter," *The Bible Knowledge Commentary*, New Testament ed., ed. John F. Walvoord and Roy B. Zuck (Wheaton, Ill.: SP Publications, Victor Books, 1983), p. 867.

Concluding Suggestions for All in the Faith

Congratulations! You've made it to the first rest stop on our climb through 2 Peter 1. Even though we've scaled only eleven verses, already we have come a long way. Before you go on to the next lesson, give yourself time to rest and reflect on two important truths. First, *living a useful life on earth begins with salvation and requires diligence.* And second, *leaving a fruitful life behind at death results in motivation for others and guarantees rewards* (see Heb. 6:10–12). These truths should give you a second wind for the ascent in our next chapter.

 Living Insights

As we read over the first eleven verses of 2 Peter, a basic theme of the letter quickly surfaces—the knowledge of God. The term *knowledge* and its related words occur a total of eleven times in 2 Peter (1:2, 3, 5, 6, 8, 20; 2:20, twice in v. 21; 3:3, 18). Let's explore this theme a little further.

Look up Jeremiah 9:23–24 and write down what it teaches about knowing God.

_____

_____

What do you learn about God from verse 24?

_____

_____

Your knowledge of God should be ever growing and evergreen, branching out and blossoming with new revelations of Him. What have you learned about God recently that you didn't know before?

_____

_____

_____

_____

_____

_____

_____

_____

Two books that might increase your knowledge of God are J. I. Packer's *Knowing God* and A. W. Tozer's *Knowledge of the Holy.* Both are excellent.

🍇 *Living Insights*   STUDY TWO

In 2 Peter 1:5–7, Peter constructs a pyramid of Christian virtues. Let's spend the next few minutes surveying his architecture.

What forms the foundation to that pyramid? _____

Why? (See Eph. 2:8 and Heb. 11:6.) _____

_____

What forms the capstone to that pyramid? _____

Why? (See 1 Cor. 13:1–13.) _____

_____

Which of the virtues listed in 2 Peter 1:5–7 is most developed in your life?

_____

Which is least developed? _____

What are a few things you could do to strengthen that quality in your life?

1. _____

2. _____

3. _____

What two benefits could we expect by beefing up our character with these qualities (see v. 8)?

1. _____

2. _____

What eternal benefit can we anticipate (v. 11)? (See also 2 Cor. 5:10 and 1 Cor. 3:10–15.)

_____

_____

Chapter 3
BE SURE OF YOUR SOURCE
2 Peter 1:12–21

A phrase some believers constantly volley back and forth is "God told me . . ." Usually the people who use this spiritual-sounding phrase don't like to be quizzed on the details of exactly *how* God spoke to them. Why? Because when you look at the source of their revelation, it often lacks either good common sense or biblical justification.

Popular Sources of "Divine Revelation"

Here's a sampling of some of the surprising ways people claim to receive a word from God.

The Natural Realm

Oftentimes what is interpreted as a revelation from God is nothing more than our own superstitions at work. Like the fellow who decided, while driving, that if the next four lights were green, then God was telling him to go to the mission field. The lights were green and the fellow went, but he didn't last two years.

Or how about the man who earnestly prayed before going on a date, "Lord, if she wears that red skirt to dinner this evening, I'll know she's the one for me." The woman wore the skirt and the man felt he had a sure word from God to marry her.

Once a woman went to sleep struggling with whether she should take a trip to Israel. When she awoke the next morning, the time on her digital clock read 7:47. Immediately she knew God was telling her to go. Why? Because the plane that was to take her was a Boeing 747.

Another popular method many use to interpret God's voice is astrology. Far from being the vice of only a few uneducated people, many Christians are now attempting to divine the will of God from the arrangement of the stars.

The Supernatural Realm

People also dabble in the supernatural realm to hear God's voice. Some claim to have dreams and visions. Others rely on spurious methods such as crystals and tarot cards. And still others turn to the occult, using mediums and channelers to allegedly contact the dead.

Why do people do this? Why are so many of us eager to follow the latest guru who claims to hear the voice of God? Primarily because of a desire to know truth. We would like to know the truth about our future, our marriages, and other major concerns in our lives. But seeking truth from traffic lights and tarot cards is not where God promises we'll find it.

Let's turn to Peter's second epistle and listen as he talks about truth—*the* truth and where we can find it.

A Personal Reminder of "The Truth"

In our last lesson, Peter exhorted us to "apply all diligence" in developing specific character qualities so that we might live useful and fruitful lives (2 Pet. 1:1–11). Now, beginning in verse 12, he addresses the subject of the truth . . . what it is and what it is not.

What It Is

Simply stated, the truth is God's revelation, His Word. Being God's children, we should establish ourselves in that truth, as Peter reminds us.

> Therefore, I shall always be ready to remind you of these things, even though you already know them, and have been established in the truth which is present with you. (v. 12)

God hasn't hidden His truth so that we must grope for it in the stars or behind superstitious feelings. He has given it to us in written form so that we might continually read, study, and apply it.

Knowing that his death is imminent, Peter wants his readers to remember that there *is* truth they can rely on.

> And I consider it right, as long as I am in this earthly dwelling, to stir you up by way of reminder, knowing that the laying aside of my earthly dwelling is imminent, as also our Lord Jesus Christ has made clear to me. And I will also be diligent that at any time after my departure you may be able to call these things to mind. (vv. 13–15)

For Peter, truth was objective, something he could leave behind with the assurance that it would provide everything pertaining to life and godliness (see 2 Tim. 3:16–17).

What It Is Not

Based on his own experience and that of the other apostles, Peter now explains what the truth is not.

> For we did not follow cleverly devised tales when we made known to you the power and coming of our Lord Jesus Christ, but we were eyewitnesses of His majesty. (v. 16)

The word *tales* comes from a Greek root which gives us our word *myth*. According to commentator Edwin A. Blum,

> The [New Testament] always uses *mythos* in a negative sense and in contrast to the truth of the gospel (1 Tim. 1:4; 4:7; 2 Tim. 4:4). . . . It is likely that the false teachers claimed that the Incarnation, Resurrection, and coming kingdom the apostles spoke about were only stories.[1]

Peter's preaching didn't rest on clever myths, as did the doctrines of the false teachers. Everything he taught concerning Christ's power and second coming came directly from his firsthand experience on the Mount of Transfiguration (Matt. 17:1–8). Peter could legitimately say, "God told me." And then the apostle repeats the direct revelation God gave him.

> For when He received honor and glory from God the Father, such an utterance as this was made to Him by the Majestic Glory, "This is My beloved Son with whom I am well-pleased"—and we ourselves heard this utterance made from heaven when we were with Him on the holy mountain. (vv. 17–18)

General Statements regarding Scripture

Recalling that unforgettable experience on the mountain sparks Peter to give us three helpful assurances concerning God's truth.

The Sure Word

The audible revelation Peter had received gave him even further assurance concerning the written words handed down by the Old Testament prophets.

---

1. Edwin A. Blum, "2 Peter," *The Expositor's Bible Commentary*, ed. Frank E. Gaebelein (Grand Rapids, Mich.: Zondervan Publishing House, Regency Reference Library, 1981), vol. 12, p. 273.

And so we have the prophetic word made more sure.
(v. 19a)

The word *prophetic* here refers to all of Scripture, not just the books or passages specifically dealing with prophecy. Peter is saying, "We have in the Old Testament an even more certain word from God than I received on that mountain." Samuel Cox wrote,

> Peter knew a sounder basis for faith than that of signs and wonders. He had seen our Lord Jesus Christ receive honor and glory from God the Father in the holy mount; he had been dazzled and carried out of himself by visions and voices from heaven; but nevertheless, even when his memory and heart are throbbing with recollections of that sublime scene, he says, "we have something surer still in the prophetic word."[2]

When we rely on sources other than Scripture for truth, we are casting our lives upon a sea of uncertainty. Feelings, circumstances, stars, these all fluctuate. And to trust in them is to open ourselves to being seriously deluded and led into error. God's written Word, however, never changes and, when properly applied, will never lead anyone into error.

The Authoritative Word

The experienced apostle then urges his readers to cultivate more than a casual reliance on God's Word.

> And so we have the prophetic word made more sure, to which you do well to pay attention as to a lamp shining in a dark place, until the day dawns and the morning star arises in your hearts. (v. 19)

The Greek term Peter uses for *dark* means "murky." The prince of darkness has turned this world, which began as a garden, into a murky swamp. And if we're to avoid becoming mired in that darkness, we must heed the light of God's Word until the Morning Star, the light of the world, returns (see Rev. 22:16 and John 8:12).

Peter then concludes his exhortation with an important explanation.

---

2. Quoted by Kenneth W. Wuest in "In These Last Days," *Wuest's Word Studies from the Greek New Testament* (Grand Rapids, Mich.: William B. Eerdmans Publishing Co., 1966), vol. 4, p. 34.

> But know this first of all, that no prophecy of Scripture is a matter of one's own interpretation. (v. 20)

Many interpret "one's" as referring to the reader of Scripture. But if that were so, it would mean that no one has a right to interpret God's truth. And yet one of the functions of the Holy Spirit is to illuminate the Word so we can interpret and apply it. So what does the apostle mean? Possibly Peter is saying that no statement from Scripture is meant to stand on its own, unrelated to the rest of Scripture. Every individual passage must be understood in light of all the rest.

Another possibility, which ties in best with the following verse, is that Peter means all Scripture originated with God and not with the writers themselves.

The Inspired Word

> For no prophecy was ever made by an act of human will, but men moved by the Holy Spirit spoke from God. (v. 21)

Unlike myths born of human authors, the Scriptures originated from God. How? The key unlocking the mystery of how fallible men could write God's infallible Word is found in the word *moved.*

> As the authors of Scripture wrote their prophecies, they were impelled or borne along by God's Spirit. What they wrote was thus inspired by God (2 Tim. 3:16). "Borne along" or "carried along" translates the word *pheromenoi.* Luke used this word in referring to a sailing vessel carried along by the wind (Acts 27:15, 17). The Scriptures' human authors were controlled by the divine Author, the Holy Spirit. Yet they were consciously involved in the process; they were neither taking dictation nor writing in a state of ecstasy.[3]

God superintended what was written, even down to the individual words used (see Matt. 5:18–19; 1 Cor. 2:12–13). He did this by using each of the biblical writers' personalities and styles of

---

3. Kenneth O. Gangel, "2 Peter," in *The Bible Knowledge Commentary,* New Testament ed., ed. John F. Walvoord and Roy B. Zuck (Wheaton, Ill.: SP Publications, Victor Books, 1983), p. 869.

writing. For example, if you read the Scriptures in their original language, you would see a great difference between the simple style of John and the scholarly style of Paul.

Like the living Word who became flesh (John 1:14), the written Word is a sure and authoritative source of truth. No wonder Satan is so determined to destroy our faith in the Word. And no wonder Peter was so determined to strengthen our faith in it.

When Seeking "A Word from God," Remember Two Things

Like Peter, we also want to stir you up by way of reminder so that you may be able to call to mind two important truths at any time in the future. First: *Remember, when you turn to God's Word, you're consulting the most reliable of all sources.* And second: *Remember, when you make other sources—experiences, dreams, feelings, stars—equal to or more reliable than the Scriptures, you will soon fall into error.*

 Living Insights

Today's lesson has been about truth, especially the sure truth of God's Word. Let's take some time now to look at what the Word of God has to say about itself.

Psalm 19:7–8 _____

Psalm 119:105 _____

Proverbs 30:5–6 _____

Isaiah 40:8 _____

Matthew 4:4 _____

Matthew 5:18 _____

Luke 24:27 _____

Romans 15:4 _____

2 Timothy 3:15 _____

2 Timothy 3:16 _____

Hebrews 4:12 _____

2 Peter 1:21 _____

Growing Deep in the Christian Life is a book on the basic beliefs taught in the Bible. In the chapter titled "God's Book—God's Voice" are some penetrating questions that would be profitable for you to ponder.

> What is your final authority in life?
> I mean, when you're cornered, when you're really up against it, when you're forced to face reality, upon what do you lean?
> Before you answer too quickly, think about it for a few moments. When it comes to establishing a standard for morality, what's your ruler? When you need an ethical compass to find your way out of an ethical jungle, where's north? When you're on a stormy, churning sea of emotions, which lighthouse shows you where to find the shore?[4]

What are some benefits of the Word of God as it relates to your own life?

Psalm 19:7 _____

v. 8 _____

v. 11 _____

Psalm 119:11 _____

v. 98 _____

v. 99 _____

v. 100 _____

Matthew 7:24–25 _____

John 8:31–32 _____

Romans 10:17 _____

2 Timothy 3:15 _____

---

4. Charles R. Swindoll, *Growing Deep in the Christian Life* (Portland, Oreg.: Multnomah Press, 1986), p. 53.

v. 16 _____

v. 17 _____

Hebrews 4:12 _____

With such wonderful benefits extended to us, it would be foolish not to lean on the Word of God as our final authority in life, wouldn't it?

For additional study in this area, the following books will be helpful:

Geisler, Norman. *Inerrancy.* Grand Rapids, Mich.: Zondervan Publishing House, 1980.

McDowell, Josh. *Evidence That Demands a Verdict.* rev. ed. San Bernardino, Calif.: Here's Life Publishers, 1979.

Pinnock, Clark H. *Biblical Revelation.* 2d ed. Phillipsburg, N.J.: Presbyterian and Reformed Publishing Co., 1985.

Swindoll, Charles R. *Growing Deep in the Christian Life.* Portland, Oreg.: Multnomah Press, 1986. See especially chapter 3, "God's Book—God's Voice."

Warfield, Benjamin B. 2d ed. *The Inspiration and Authority of the Bible.* Phillipsburg, N.J.: Presbyterian and Reformed Publishing Co., 1948.

Chapter 4

AN EXPOSÉ OF COUNTERFEIT COMMUNICATORS

2 Peter 2:1–3

Sooner or later we all get conned at least once. Perhaps you've been bamboozled by a forgery or a bogus investment scheme. Maybe you lost only your spare change; maybe it was your life savings. Or perhaps it nearly cost you your sanity, as it did Christopher Edwards. Listen to what he writes in the foreword to his book *Crazy for God.*

> This book is about the rapid near-destruction of a human being—myself. It is the story of the deceit, manipulation and terror which thousands of young Americans experience daily at the hands of modern cults. . . .
>
> My story began innocently enough when I was lured into a "fun" weekend in June of 1975 on a farm owned by a front group for Sun Myung Moon's Unification Church. . . .
>
> . . . I was transformed from an intelligent, independent human being into a completely subservient disciple of my new Messiah—terrified of questioning, dependent on my leaders for my every move, ready and willing to die or even kill to restore the world under the absolute rule of Reverend Moon. . . . [In this book] I describe my losing battle to retain my mind and will in a world of structured madness.[1]

Of all the cons we can fall prey to, one of the worst is being duped by a religious phony. Swindlers of this kind deal in counterfeit truth—something that looks and sounds right but is actually contrary to fact, an imitation meant to deceive the unsuspecting. These

---

1. Christopher Edwards, *Crazy for God* (Englewood Cliffs, N.J.: Prentice-Hall, 1979), foreword.

cons don't happen just on farms, and they aren't always done for the benefit of some leader whose name you can't pronounce. No, every week, lies dressed up in their Sunday best receive nodding approval in mainline churches everywhere. Counterfeit truth is big business, and it's still owned and operated by the same insidious proprietor who began it all years ago in a garden.

The Original Counterfeit

In 2 Corinthians 11, Paul writes about the world's first con artist, his methods, and his goal.

> I am afraid, lest as the serpent deceived Eve by his craftiness, your minds should be led astray from the simplicity and purity of devotion to Christ. (v. 3)

Who Is He?

This "serpent" Paul writes of is the original imposter, Satan. Jesus described him as one who

> "does not stand in the truth, because there is no truth in him. Whenever he speaks a lie, he speaks from his own nature; for he is a liar, and the father of lies." (John 8:44b)

What Does He Do?

First of all, Satan is in the deception business—"the serpent deceived Eve by his craftiness" (2 Cor. 11:3a). He's a master at lying, and he makes it his business to know his subjects' weaknesses so that he can exploit them, just as he did Eve's.

Second, Satan's target is always the mind—"minds . . . led astray" (v. 3b). Because once the mind has been duped into believing a lie, the emotions will follow. And what's Satan's goal? To lead us "from the simplicity and purity of devotion to Christ" (v. 3c).

Third, Paul warns that Satan isn't in the habit of placing his repulsively wicked side on public display very often. Instead, he "disguises himself as an angel of light" (v. 14) and subtly substitutes his lies for God's truth. With his power of deception, Satan can make even lies sound as if they were gloriously inspired and worthy of our belief.

Fourth, Satan doesn't do everything himself; he delegates his tasks and uses others to counterfeit the truth and accomplish his goals.

Therefore it is not surprising if his servants also disguise themselves as servants of righteousness; whose end shall be according to their deeds. (v. 15)

Like their master, these individuals will seem doctrinally sound, caring, and worthy of your support. But what they're actually offering is a false righteousness, a false Messiah, and a false hope for eternity. Jesus reserved some of his most scorching words for these kinds of people.

"Woe to you, scribes and Pharisees, hypocrites, because you travel about on sea and land to make one proselyte; and when he becomes one, you make him twice as much a son of hell as yourselves." (Matt. 23:15)

A Portrait of False Leaders

The apostle Peter also had some things to say about religious leaders who peddled false teachings. In the first three verses of 2 Peter 2, he provides us with four telling characteristics of counterfeit communicators.

. . . There will also be false teachers among you, who will secretly introduce destructive heresies, even denying the Master who bought them, bringing swift destruction upon themselves. And many will follow their sensuality, and because of them the way of the truth will be maligned; and in their greed they will exploit you with false words. (2 Peter 2:1–3a)

First: *Religious phonies deceitfully present heresy* (v. 1). Not only are their teachings false, they're "destructive." The false doctrines introduced into the body of Christ are like a malignant cancer; they will either destroy or be destroyed. There can be no peaceful coexistence between falsehood and God's truth.

The method used for introducing falsehood is revealed in the word *heresy*. In Greek it conveys the idea of "making a choice." False teachers want to force us to choose between their teaching and that of orthodox Christianity. But their style is not offensive. They won't blatantly deny the truth, in the beginning. Instead, as Warren Wiersbe notes,

they simply lay their false teachings alongside the truth and give the impression that they believe the

30

fundamentals of the faith. Before long, they remove the true doctrine and leave their false doctrine in its place.[2]

Religious counterfeits are also masters of what Peter calls "false words" (v. 3a). From the Greek term for "false," *plastos*, we get our word *plastic*. Wiersbe adds,

> Plastic words! Words that can be twisted to mean anything you want them to mean! The false teachers use our vocabulary, but they do not use our dictionary. They talk about "salvation," "inspiration," and the great words of the Christian faith, but they do not mean what we mean.[3]

Second: *They openly deny the truth* (v. 1). False teachers are better known for what they *deny* than for what they embrace. Their teaching is peppered with denials of God's Word instead of salted with affirmations of the truth. They deny the verbal inspiration of the Scriptures, the sinfulness of humanity, the deity of Christ, the blood atonement of Christ on the cross, the resurrection of Christ, salvation by grace through faith alone, the presence and activity of a literal devil, Christ's second coming, and the other foundational truths Christianity rests upon.

Are such people saved? According to what Peter writes in this chapter, no, they're not. They "deny the Master who bought them" and face a "swift destruction" (v. 1), and they are "slaves of corruption" (v. 19a). But how can someone whom the Lord "bought" (v. 1) not be saved? Doesn't the blood of Christ atone for all sin?

It's true that Christ's death on the cross paid for the sins of the whole world—including false teachers (1 John 2:2). But when it comes to *application*, the benefit of our Lord's death is limited to those who believe (John 3:16–18).

Third: *They unashamedly model sensuality* (v. 2). The Greek word used here for *sensuality* is an extremely vivid term for blatant immorality. William Barclay says it "describes the attitude of a man who is lost to shame; he is past the stage of wishing to conceal his sin and of being ashamed of it."[4]

---

2. Warren W. Wiersbe, *Be Alert* (Wheaton, Ill.: SP Publications, Victor Books, 1984), p. 38.

3. Wiersbe, *Be Alert*, p. 38.

4. William Barclay, *The Letters of James and Peter*, 2d ed., The Daily Study Bible Series (Philadelphia, Pa.: Westminster Press, 1960), p. 377.

Now we can understand the reasoning behind the deceitful workers' denial of the truth. In order for them to pursue their lusts under the guise of Christianity, they must redefine God's standard of righteousness. The subtle ridiculing of "Victorian morals" is an attempt to discredit God's holiness and promote their own standard of sensuality as wholesome and acceptable.

How do they accomplish this? By promoting a counterfeit form of grace. For the believer, grace means being freed from sin to obey Christ (see Rom. 6). To the deceiver, grace is twisted to mean freedom to do as one pleases.

This twisted position on grace results in two things. To begin with, the deceivers get a big following. Anyone who promotes this type of counterfeit grace will be instantly popular. In addition, the deceivers and their followers will bring a reproach on the name of Christ (v. 2b).

Fourth: *They selfishly represent greed* (v. 3). Did you notice the word *exploit?* In Greek, the word is *pleoxonexia; pleon* means "more," and *exia* comes from the verb which means "to have." It's a covetous desire for money, lust for another person, or an unholy ambition for honor, prestige, or power. These are the motives behind the false teachers and their teachings.

Warning flags should go up in our minds every time teachers overemphasize that we buy their books, songs, and tapes. True ministers of the gospel don't follow Christ for money; and they also don't flatter, cater to the wealthy, demand unquestioning loyalty, or play around with lust. All these are the marks of greedy frauds who exploit their followers.

Well, that's plenty to think about, isn't it? Let's summarize what we've learned to make it easier to remember. *Number one:* False teachers appear to embrace orthodoxy and encourage you to think, but in reality it's a counterfeit message. They are deceitfully presenting heresy. *Number two:* False teachers appear to stand firm on truth, but in reality it's a counterfeit stance. They're actually denying biblical truth. *Number three:* False teachers appear to be those who love the doctrine of grace and our life of freedom for the glory of Christ, but it's a counterfeit grace. In reality, sensuality is being modeled and shameless lust is at work. *Number four:* False teachers appear to have our good at heart, but theirs is a counterfeit sincerity. In reality, greed is their motivation.

Some Tips on Spotting the Spurious

Now that we know counterfeit communicators are out there, how can we be sure that what's being taught on the radio, TV, or in our local churches is truth? How can we avoid being hoodwinked by one of Satan's workers of deceit?

Here are three practical tips that can help all of us avoid being duped: *stop, look,* and *listen.*

Stop: Refuse to blindly accept someone else's teaching just because others have been "blessed" by it. Stop long enough to make a serious study, comparing what is being taught with what the Scriptures teach.

Look: Take a careful look at the life of the main spokesperson. Are the fruits of the Spirit evident—humility, love, self-control? Or is what you're seeing more the marks of a counterfeit—greed, sensuality, and dissension (see Gal. 5:19–23)? Don't be wowed because someone sounds intelligent or wooed because of someone's charisma.

Listen: Pay attention to the terms a person uses and how they're defined. Also listen to what's *not* being said. Don't judge truth just by how you feel; think, and make your judgments according to what the Scriptures teach.

In his book *Waiting,* Ben Patterson writes,

> The American Banking Association once sponsored a two-week training program to help tellers detect counterfeit bills. The program was unique—never during the two-week training did the tellers even look at a counterfeit bill, nor did they listen to any lectures concerning the characteristics of counterfeit bills. . . . All they did for two weeks was handle authentic currency, hour after hour and day after day, until they were so familiar with the true that they could not possibly be fooled by the false.[5]

That's the right approach in spotting counterfeit communicators as well. We need to study, meditate on, and apply God's Word until we are so familiar with it that we cannot be fooled by anything less than real truth.

5. Ben Patterson, *Waiting* (Downers Grove, Ill.: InterVarsity Press, 1989), p. 153.

Just as bank tellers need a thorough knowledge of legitimate currency in order to spot counterfeit bills, so Christians need a thorough knowledge of the Bible in order to spot bogus religious teaching. How grounded are you in the Scriptures? How deep are your theological roots? How capable are you of detecting false teaching?

OK, close your Bibles. Pop quiz. Below are ten major areas of doctrine. State in a sentence or two what the Bible says about each. Then, from memory, jot down a central Scripture that supports your statements.

The Bible

_____

_____

_____

Supporting Scripture: _____

God the Father

_____

_____

_____

Supporting Scripture: _____

The Lord Jesus Christ

_____

_____

_____

Supporting Scripture: _____

The Holy Spirit

_____

_____

_____

Supporting Scripture: _____

The Depravity of Humanity

_____

_____

_____

Supporting Scripture: _____

Salvation

_____

_____

_____

Supporting Scripture: _____

The Return of Christ

_____

_____

_____

Supporting Scripture: _____

The Resurrection

_____

_____

_____

Supporting Scripture: _____

The Body of Christ

_____

_____

_____

Supporting Scripture: _____

How did you do on the pop quiz? Could you use a little refresher course on the basics of biblical truth? If so, we would like to recommend a course of study that should sharpen your thinking and, hopefully, your faith.

First, nothing is more important than daily time in the Word of God. To help you get into the Word, we would like to suggest an independent study project. Tyndale Publishers has formatted an excellent reading program to take you through the Scriptures in a year. It's called the *One Year Bible,* and it's a great tool to reacquaint you with some of those books in your Bible that may have been gathering dust.

Second, we recommend Max Anders' book *30 Days to Understanding the Bible.* It provides daily studies and quizzes to strengthen your grasp on the Scriptures.

Third, for a more in-depth doctrinal study, get Chuck Swindoll's *Growing Deep in the Christian Life.* It teaches the major doctrines of the faith in a brisk and refreshingly applicable way.

Finally, if you want to be able to spot the errors in false teaching, pick up a copy of *Scripture Twisting* by James W. Sire. It shows twenty ways that the cults misread and misapply the Bible, and it can strengthen your skills of discernment.

Chapter 5
THE GOD OF WRATH AND RESCUE
2 Peter 2:4–11

Counterfeit money is deceptive because it looks so much like the real thing. Counterfeit religions share the same deception. Often their doctrinal currency looks so much like Christianity's that it is impossible to tell them apart—at least to the untrained eye.

What Peter tries to do in chapter 2 is train our eyes so that we might spot the bogus bills of heresy before they are widely circulated within the church. Not an easy task. The second-century church father Irenaeus explains why.

> Error, indeed, is never set forth in its naked deformity, lest, being thus exposed, it should at once be detected. But it is craftily decked out in an attractive dress, so as, by its outward form, to make it appear to the inexperienced . . . more true than truth itself.[1]

Developing a skill to distinguish truth from error is an arduous process of education.

> The student of cultism then, must be prepared to scale the language barrier of terminology. First, he must recognize that it does exist, and second, he must acknowledge the very real fact that unless terms are defined . . . the semantic jungle which the cults have created will envelop him, making difficult, if not impossible, a proper contrast between the teaching of the cults and those of orthodox Christianity.[2]

Before we turn to 2 Peter, let's look at two very different, yet absolutely reliable, facts about God.

---

1. As quoted by D. R. McConnell in *A Different Gospel* (Peabody, Mass.: Hendrickson Publishers, 1988), p. xiii.

2. Walter R. Martin, *The Kingdom of the Cults*, rev. ed. (Minneapolis, Minn.: Bethany Fellowship, Inc., Publishers, 1968), p. 18.

Two Sides of the Same God

One of those facts was written by Jeremiah as he wandered through the ruins of Jerusalem. Stumbling over the rubble, he fell on his face before the Lord and cried out in despair (Lam. 3:1–20). What lifted him up was a memory—a memory of *God's compassion.*

> This I recall to my mind,
> Therefore I have hope.
> The Lord's lovingkindnesses indeed never cease,
> For His compassions never fail.
> They are new every morning;
> Great is Thy faithfulness. (vv. 21–23)

This is the picture we all want to hang over the mantle—the one of a loving Father who sends forth His kindness as faithfully and fulgently as the sun sends out its rays to brighten the morning. That picture of God is boldly framed in the Scriptures. But there is also another picture—one that we would prefer to hang in some infrequently trafficked hallway. It is the picture of *God's judgment.*

After a lengthy exposé of human sin in Romans 1, Paul informs us that God is not a "boys-will-be-boys" type of deity; He is a God of righteousness, wrath, and judgment.

> Therefore you are without excuse, every man of you who passes judgment, for in that you judge another, you condemn yourself; for you who judge practice the same things. And we know that the judgment of God rightly falls upon those who practice such things. And do you suppose this, O man, when you pass judgment upon those who practice such things and do the same yourself, that you will escape the judgment of God? (Rom. 2:1–3)

God does not look the other way when it comes to depravity. He takes sin into account with fine-point accuracy. One day He will open His ledger of human conduct for a day of reckoning, and the bills of bankrupt lives will come due.

> It is appointed for men to die once and after this comes judgment. (Heb. 9:27)

Interestingly, these two sides of God, compassion and judgment, come together in a composite picture in 2 Peter 2:4–11.

Judging the Wicked

At the height of the Roman Empire, with its expansive network of highways, it was said that all roads lead to Rome. In today's labyrinth of religions, it is said that all roads lead to heaven. Of course, they don't.[3] Peter gives a few examples of those who have taken a wrong turn, a turn that leads straight to hell.

Sinning Angels

> God did not spare angels when they sinned, but cast them into hell and committed them to pits of darkness, reserved for judgment. (v. 4)

When Lucifer plummeted from his exalted position before God, numerous angels fell with him, some of whom were involved in earthly perversions (compare Jude 6 with Gen. 6:4). These defecting angels have been cast into a kind of death row[4] where they await their final judgment in the lake of fire (Rev. 20). For these sinning angels there will be no dawn of lovingkindness from heaven. Morning by morning new mercies will not be theirs to see. Their doom will only grow darker as their destiny draws nearer.

Ungodly Humanity

There were others, besides the sinning angels, whom "God did not spare": unbelievers who rejected Noah's message (Gen. 6–7) and the wicked inhabitants of Sodom and Gomorrah (Gen. 19). Both groups are referred to in 2 Peter 2:5–6.

---

3. See Matthew 7:13–14 and John 14:6.

4. "There are three Greek words that are translated 'hell' in the NT of KJV. The first is *geenna* (Gehenna), which really means 'hell' and is so rendered in almost all versions. . . . Gehenna was the Valley of the Son of Hinnom, south of Jerusalem. Ahaz and Manasseh, two wicked kings of Judah, sacrificed their sons there to the heathen god Molech (2 Chron. 28:3; 33:6; Jer. 32:35). Good King Josiah defiled the place (2 Kings 23:10), and it became the city dump, with fires burning on it. Then the Jews made 'Gehenna' the name for the final judgment and the place of eternal punishment. Jesus used it that way (11 times). The second word translated 'hell' in the NT (KJV) is *hades*. . . . *Hades* was the name of the god of the underworld and does not mean the place of everlasting punishment; so it should not be translated 'hell.' It is used in the NT for the abode of departed spirits. . . . Here in 2 Pet. 2:4 we find the third word, *tartarosas* (only here in NT). . . . The verb comes from the noun *tartaros*, used for the dark abode of the wicked dead. In the apocryphal Book of Enoch (20:2) it is used as the place of punishment of the fallen angels (as here in 2 Peter). In English we use the Latin form 'Tartarus.'" Ralph Earle, *Word Meanings in the New Testament* (Grand Rapids, Mich.: Baker Book House, 1986), pp. 446–47.

[God] did not spare the ancient world, but preserved Noah, a preacher of righteousness, with seven others, when He brought a flood upon the world of the ungodly; and . . . He condemned the cities of Sodom and Gomorrah to destruction by reducing them to ashes, having made them an example to those who would live ungodly thereafter.

Skipping down to the second half of verse 9, Peter concludes from these specific examples that "the Lord knows how . . . to keep the unrighteous under punishment for the day of judgment."

Just as God did not overlook the sin of Sodom and Gomorrah or the perversion of the antediluvian world, so He will not overlook the error of today's false teachers. And how will He deal with these heretics? He will keep them under punishment, reserved for the day of judgment, as illustrated by the example Jesus gave in Luke 16:23–31.

"In Hades he lifted up his eyes, being in torment, and saw Abraham far away, and Lazarus in his bosom. And he cried out and said, 'Father Abraham, have mercy on me, and send Lazarus, that he may dip the tip of his finger in water and cool off my tongue; for I am in agony in this flame.' But Abraham said, 'Child, remember that during your life you received your good things, and likewise Lazarus bad things; but now he is being comforted here, and you are in agony. And besides all this, between us and you there is a great chasm fixed, in order that those who wish to come over from here to you may not be able, and that none may cross over from there to us.' And he said, 'Then I beg you, Father, that you send him to my father's house—for I have five brothers—that he may warn them, lest they also come to this place of torment.' But Abraham said, 'They have Moses and the Prophets; let them hear them.' But he said, 'No, Father Abraham, but if someone goes to them from the dead, they will repent!' But he said to him, 'If they do not listen to Moses and the Prophets, neither will they be persuaded if someone rises from the dead.'"

When an unbeliever dies, the body remains in the grave while the soul goes to Hades. There it remains in some state of torment, as described in Luke 16, until the final resurrection. For the believer, this is a glorious entrance into eternal bliss (see 1 Cor. 15:51-55).[5] But for the unbeliever, it is a grim exit into eternal banishment.[6]

> I saw a great white throne and Him who sat upon it, from whose presence earth and heaven fled away, and no place was found for them. And I saw the dead, the great and the small, standing before the throne, and books were opened; and another book was opened, which is the book of life; and the dead were judged from the things which were written in the books, according to their deeds. And the sea gave up the dead which were in it, and death and Hades gave up the dead which were in them; and they were judged, every one of them according to their deeds. And death and Hades were thrown into the lake of fire. This is the second death, the lake of fire. And if anyone's name was not found written in the book of life, he was thrown into the lake of fire. (Rev. 20:11–15)

First Peter 1:3–5 promises the believer an escape from such a future. Not only is there rescue from judgment in the future, but as 2 Peter 2 informs us, there is rescue here and now from temptation.

Rescuing the Righteous

In the midst of the historic judgments upon the unrighteous, there was also the dramatic rescue of the righteous; each story of destruction also told a story of deliverance. God reached into the desperate ranks of humanity and cupped His merciful hands around the hearts that belonged to Him.

---

5. "When death takes place, the soul and spirit depart immediately into the presence of the Lord. . . . When the body is resurrected, the soul and spirit will be joined to that glorified body. . . . And in this glorified state, we will spend eternity with our God. . . . Every believer in Jesus Christ who goes home to be with the Lord has this unshakable and marvelous future in front of him or her." Chuck Swindoll, *Growing Deep in the Christian Life* (Portland, Oreg.: Multnomah Press, 1986), p. 303.

6. In spite of the severe sentences God has meted out on the unrighteous, He does not wish "for any to perish but for all to come to repentance" (2 Pet. 3:9; see also 1 Tim. 2:4).

Preserving Noah

God not only preserved Noah and his family from the spiritual destruction that was caused by the corruption covering the earth, He also preserved them from the physical destruction that came as a consequence. In the same manner, the Lord Jesus Christ will deliver us and shelter us from the wrath to come (1 Thess. 5:9).

Protecting Lot

Just as God preserved Noah and his family from the Flood, so He protected Lot and his family from the fire and brimstone that rained down upon Sodom and Gomorrah.

> And if He condemned the cities of Sodom and Gomorrah to destruction by reducing them to ashes, having made them an example to those who would live ungodly thereafter; and if He rescued righteous Lot, oppressed by the sensual conduct of unprincipled men (for by what he saw and heard that righteous man, while living among them, felt his righteous soul tormented day after day with their lawless deeds), then the Lord knows how to rescue the godly from temptation, and to keep the unrighteous under punishment for the day of judgment, and especially those who indulge the flesh in its corrupt desires and despise authority. Daring, self-willed, they do not tremble when they revile angelic majesties, whereas angels who are greater in might and power do not bring a reviling judgment against them before the Lord. (2 Pet. 2:6–11)

The story of Lot, Abraham's nephew, begins in Genesis 13, where he was given a choice of where to pasture his animals. He chose the fertile meadows in the valley of the Jordan, which led him to the commercial centers of Sodom and Gomorrah. These twin cities were also the center of gross immorality (see Gen. 18:20). Homosexuality ran rampant through the streets (19:1–9), and not even as many as ten righteous people lived there (18:23–32; 19:13).

How did living in a moral cesspool affect Lot? Peter says it oppressed and tormented him. But hints in the biblical narrative indicate a few calluses on the otherwise sensitive surface of Lot's soul; for when God sent angels of deliverance to escort him out of town, he hesitated. So the men seized his hand and the hand of his wife and the hands of his daughters, for the compassion of the Lord was upon him; and they brought him out, and put him outside the city. (v. 16)

Notice the word that we saw earlier in Lamentations 3:22: *compassion*. The Hebrew word is *chamal*. It means "to spare or to have compassion on."

Basically, this root connotes that emotional response which results (or may result) in action to remove its object . . . from impending difficulty.[7]

Two Facts for Us to Remember

In conclusion, we want to underscore two vital facts that are essential to remember.

Number one: *God's compassion will result in the rescue of all believers.* His heart goes out to us as He stoops in compassion to extricate us from whatever moral morass we find ourselves trapped in (see 1 Cor. 10:13).

Number two: *God's judgment will result in the punishment of all unbelievers.* Those who die without Christ as their Savior will face not the loving embrace of a heavenly Father but the judicial impartiality of a righteous Judge. For Christians, eternal condemnation is behind them, but for non-Christians, it looms before them.

Living Insights STUDY ONE

Today's text unfolds like a bolt of dark cloth, revealing the seamless continuity of God's judgment in history. But running through that fabric is the thread of His compassion. That thread passes through the lineage of Noah and Lot and extends to the remnant of the righteous today.

What trial or temptation have *you* recently gone through?

_____

_____

7. *Theological Wordbook of the Old Testament*, ed. R. Laird Harris, Gleason L. Archer, Jr., and Bruce K. Waltke (Chicago, Ill.: Moody Press, 1980), vol. 1, p. 296.

How did God rescue you from it?

_____

_____

_____

What is one way He rescues us during times like that (see
1 Cor. 10:13)?

_____

What is another way (see James 5:11)?

_____

🍇 *Living Insights* STUDY TWO

When we talk about God keeping "the unrighteous under punishment for the day of judgment" (2 Pet. 2:9b), it's easy to become
cerebral about their fate and to chart the chronology of God's
judgment—the Tribulation . . . the Great White Throne . . . the
lake of fire—with a certain emotional detachment. Regarding this
breach of the heart, A. W. Tozer writes:

> It is not a reassuring thought that the writings
> of the grief-stricken prophets are often pored over by
> persons whose interests are curious merely and who
> never shed one tear for the woes of the world. . . .
> Whatever is done without heart is done in the
> dark no matter how scriptural it may appear to be.[8]

What's even worse than being unconcerned about the condemned is being glib about their fate. British theologian John Stott
admonishes us about this serious error in our emotions.

> I want to repudiate with all the vehemence of
> which I am capable the glibness, what almost ap-
> pears to be the glee . . . with which some Evangeli-
> cals speak about hell. It is a horrible sickness of

8. A. W. Tozer, *God Tells the Man Who Cares* (Harrisburg, Pa.: Christian Publications, 1970),
pp. 9–10, 11.

mind or spirit. Instead, since on the day of judgement, when some will be condemned, there is going to be 'weeping and gnashing of teeth' (Matthew 8:12; 22:13; 24:51; 25:30; Luke 13:28), should we not already begin to weep at the very prospect? I thank God for Jeremiah . . . charged with the heartbreaking mission of prophesying the destruction of his nation. Its ruin would only be temporary; it would not be eternal. Nevertheless, he could not restrain his tears. 'Oh that my head were a spring of water and my eyes a fountain of tears! I would weep day and night for the slain of my people' (Jeremiah 9:1; cf. 13:17; 14:17).

It is within this prophetic tradition of tragedy, of sorrow over people's rejection of God's word and over the resultant inevitability of judgement, that Jesus wept over the impenitent city of Jerusalem. He cried out: 'If you, even you, had only known on this day what would bring you peace . . . !' (Luke 19:41–42; cf. Matthew 23:37–38). In this too Paul had the mind of Christ. He was willing even, like Moses before him, to be himself 'cursed and cut off from Christ' if only thereby his people might be saved (Romans 9:1–4; 10:1; cf. Exodus 32:32). He had the same deep feelings for the Gentiles. . . . (Acts 20:31; cf. 20:19; Philippians 3:18).

I long that we could in some small way stand in the tearful tradition of Jeremiah, Jesus and Paul. I want to see more tears among us. I think we need to repent of our nonchalance, our hard-heartedness.[9]

If, after reading and meditating on these two quotations, God's Spirit has convicted you about a lack of compassion for the condemned, now would be a good time to repent and pray for a change of heart. As you pray, reflect on this additional thought from Tozer:

Those Christian leaders who shook the world were one and all men of sorrows whose witness to mankind welled out of heavy hearts.[10]

9. David L. Edwards and John Stott, *Evangelical Essentials* (Downers Grove, Ill.: InterVarsity Press, 1988), pp. 312–13.

10. Tozer, *God Tells the Man Who Cares*, p. 9.

Chapter 6

DISOBEDIENCE GONE TO SEED

2 Peter 2:12–19

After interviewing some fifteen thousand tiny guests on his "House Party" show in the 1950s, Art Linkletter compiled his funniest interviews in a book titled *Kids Say the Darndest Things!* Here's a sample of the guileless anecdotes that came from the mouths of those fidgeting and unflinchingly honest babes.

> *What does your mom do?*
> She's a Sunday School teacher.
> *What does she do for fun?*
> She plays poker and drinks beer. . . .

> And what about the innocent who spouted: "My Dad's a cop who arrests burglars, robbers and thieves."
> When I said, "Doesn't your mother worry about such a risky job?" he answered, "Naw, she thinks it's a great job. He brings home rings, and bracelets and jewelry almost every week."[1]

Oops. It was forthright exchanges like these, along with thousands of unexpected others, that taught Mr. Linkletter this interesting insight:

> Children under ten and women over seventy give the best interviews . . . for the identical reason: They speak the plain unvarnished truth. They dish it out in no uncertain terms, with heartfelt emotion coloring each phrase.
> No concealing, flattering, hypocritical editorializing among the very young and very old! If you don't want the truth—better not ask them![2]

---

1. Art Linkletter, *Kids Say the Darndest Things!* (Englewood Cliffs, N.J.: Prentice-Hall, 1957), pp. 63, 54.

2. Linkletter, *Kids Say the Darndest Things*, p. 1.

There's someone else we'd better not ask if we don't want the truth. Someone whose book we'd better not read if we're wanting to be pampered and protected from reality. If you don't want the plain unvarnished truth—better not read God's Word!

God Tells the Truth about Everything

When God directed the writers of Scripture, He never once whispered, "Now, go easy on this, we don't want to offend anyone." Instead, He made sure that His book would contain nothing but the unvarnished truth about everything and everybody.

Take David, for example. As great as his faith and life were, God didn't hedge when it came to telling the truth about his adulterous affair with Bathsheba (2 Sam. 11). Nor was the truth hidden about Gehazi, Elisha's faithful servant, who forsook God to satisfy a lust for material possessions (2 Kings 5:20–27). And what about the two sides of King Uzziah's life story? Crowned king of Israel at sixteen, he was faithful to God, won battles, built cities, and enjoyed great fame and wealth. But God also reveals that Uzziah later acted corruptly out of pride and died a leper (2 Chron. 26).

The truth of God's Word extends not only to human lives but also to the human heart—and the diagnosis isn't good. According to Jeremiah 17:9, the heart is deceitful and desperately sick. Just how sick is presented rather bluntly by the apostle Paul in Romans 3.

> "There is none righteous, not even one;
> There is none who understands,
> There is none who seeks for God;
> All have turned aside, together they have become
>   useless;
> There is none who does good,
> There is not even one."
> "Their throat is an open grave,
> With their tongues they keep deceiving,"
> "The poison of asps is under their lips";
> "Whose mouth is full of cursing and bitterness";
> "Their feet are swift to shed blood,
> Destruction and misery are in their paths,
> And the path of peace have they not known."
> "There is no fear of God before their eyes."
> (vv. 10–18)

As severe as this passage is, today's section of God's Word will be even more unsparing. We're about to go beyond the bold lines of depravity penned by Paul to some ugly details inked in by the apostle Peter. Commentator John Henry Jowett graphically describes 2 Peter 2 as "dark and appalling."

> There is nothing quite like it elsewhere in the entire book. The misery and desolation of it are unrelieved. It is so like some wide and soddened moor, in a night of cold and drizzling rain, made lurid now and again by lightning-flash and weird with the growl of rolling thunder. Everywhere is the black and treacherous bog. The moral pollution is overwhelming. . . . The descriptive language is intense, violent, terrific [sic]. There is no softening of the shade from end to end. It begins in the denunciation of "lascivious doings"; it continues through "pits of darkness," "lawless deeds," "lust of defilement," "spots and blemishes," "children of cursing"; and it ends in the gruesome figure of "the dog turning to his own vomit and the sow that had washed to wallowing in the mire."[3]

So prepare to wade through the dregs of depravity in the second half of 2 Peter 2.

Peter Writes the Truth about Apostates

Leading into Peter's description of unchecked depravity are verses 10–11, which talk about the proud who despise authority, indulge in the flesh, and revile angelic majesties. Believe it or not, these reckless individuals are only bush league compared to the wild bunch we're about to meet. In verses 12–19 Peter introduces an even more manifestly depraved group with the two words, "But these . . ." (v. 12).

Looking Impressive, They Are Depraved

> But these, like unreasoning animals, born as creatures of instinct to be captured and killed, reviling where they have no knowledge, will in the destruction of those creatures also be destroyed, suffering

3. J. H. Jowett, *The Epistles of St. Peter* (London, England: Hodder and Stoughton, 1906), pp. 279–80.

wrong as the wages of doing wrong. They count it
a pleasure to revel in the daytime. They are stains
and blemishes, reveling in their deceptions, as they
carouse with you, having eyes full of adultery and
that never cease from sin, enticing unstable souls,
having a heart trained in greed, accursed children.
(vv. 12–14)

That's unvarnished truth, raw details of people driven like animals
by depraved appetites. People like these have hearts that are filled
with adulterous thoughts toward every person they meet. Their eyes
constantly search for the naive, the weak, the "unstable" whom
they can entice with a feigned love that is really lust in disguise.

Peter also describes these individuals as having hearts "trained
in greed" (v. 14). The New International Version translates it, "they
are experts in greed." They are masters at knowing how to jerk the
heart strings that control the purse strings.

Interestingly, those who live this kind of life have been duped into
believing that it leads to fulfillment. But, as William Barclay writes,
they are actually being led away from fulfillment to destruction.

There is something self-destroying in fleshly pleasure. To make such pleasure the be-all and the end-
all of life is in the end a suicidal policy. . . . If a
man dedicates himself to these fleshly pleasures, if
he makes them his only joy, . . . he ruins his health,
wrecks his constitution, destroys his mind and character, and begins his experience of hell when he is
still upon earth.[4]

Forsaking Truth, They Go Astray

When we interrupted Peter's thoughts earlier at the end of verse
14, he had just described these people as "accursed children." Let's
find out why.

Forsaking the right way they have gone astray, having followed the way of Balaam, the son of Beor,
who loved the wages of unrighteousness, but he received a rebuke for his own transgression; for a dumb

---

4. William Barclay, *The Letters of James and Peter*, 2d ed., The Daily Study Bible Series
(Philadelphia, Pa.: Westminster Press, 1960), p. 391.

donkey, speaking with a voice of a man, restrained
the madness of the prophet. (vv. 15–16)

The term Peter uses here for *forsaking* actually means "abandoned." They abandoned God's way to follow in Balaam's footsteps. Balaam was a hireling prophet who knew the right way but abandoned it because of a greed for money (see Num. 22–24; 31:1–16). Covetous people always have a price at which they would be willing to stray from the truth. Peter describes this kind of attitude as "madness," insane thinking. Then he uses three vivid word pictures to characterize their lives.

These are springs without water, and mists driven
by a storm, for whom the black darkness has been
reserved. (2 Peter 2:17)

First, Peter describes them as "springs without water." They look like the real thing, but they're actually only a mirage; they cannot slake spiritual thirst. Second, they sound like they have something to offer, but they're empty, like a thunderstorm that passes by without giving the expected rain, only mists. Third, they promise the light of fulfillment and joy, but their end is only blackness and gloom.

Promising Freedom, They Are Enslaved

Though these people have nothing to offer, somehow they are still able to allure others.

For speaking out arrogant words of vanity they entice
by fleshly desires, by sensuality, those who barely
escape from the ones who live in error, promising
them freedom while they themselves are slaves of
corruption; for by what a man is overcome, by this
he is enslaved. (vv. 18–19)

False teachers in particular allure others by the use of words. Warren Wiersbe writes,

They know how to impress people with their vocabulary, "inflated words that say nothing" (literal translation). . . .
Do not be impressed with religious oratory. Apollos was a fervent and eloquent religious speaker, but he did not know the right message to preach (Acts 18:24–28). Paul was careful not to build his

converts' faith on either his words or his wisdom (1 Cor. 2:1–5). Paul was a brilliant man, but his ministry was simple and practical. He preached to *express* and not to *impress.* He knew the difference between *communication* and *manipulation.*[5]

A particularly favorite word or idea apostates like to use is *freedom.* To them it means the liberty to sin as much as they like. And for those who believe this false teaching, they, like their teachers, become slaves to their own lusts.

We Are to Live the Truth . . . No Matter What

Again, John Henry Jowett's pen comes alive:

> A man's thought determines the moral climate of his life, and will settle the question whether his conduct is to be poisonous marsh or fertile meadow, fragrant garden or barren sand. The pose of the mind determines the dispositions, and will settle whether a man shall soar with angels in the heavenlies or wallow with the sow in the mire.[6]

Now that we have waded through the poisonous marsh of the apostate's life, let's finish by focusing on how we can live the truth and be "a fragrance of Christ to God" (2 Cor. 2:15a).

First: *Walk close with God.* Cultivate an open relationship with the Lord. Talk with Him daily about your fears, your burdens, and your hopes. Wait on Him, and learn to fellowship with Him through praise and worship.

Second: *Heed the counsel of His Word.* Pay attention to the wisdom of God's Word more than to any teacher. Take what He has written seriously; pay attention to His warnings.

Third: *Respect the promptings of your heart.* Anyone walking closely with God and taking His Word seriously will be given illumination from the Spirit. For example, if you are walking closely with God and feel reluctant concerning a certain leader or teacher, then honor that and hold back. Or if you sense that something is being taken to an extreme, it may well be that the Spirit is trying to keep you in balance. Learn to respect the Holy Spirit's restraint.

5. Warren W. Wiersbe, *Be Alert* (Wheaton, Ill.: SP Publications, Victor Books, 1984), p. 66.

6. Jowett, *The Epistles of St. Peter,* pp. 280–81.

Someone once said,

> Sow a thought, reap an act. Sow an act, reap a
> habit. Sow a habit, reap your character. Sow your
> character, reap your destiny.

No one wakes up one morning and decides to be a vile apostate.
Not even those individuals Peter has been describing. What we will
be like on any given morning is determined by the seed thoughts
we have sown in our hearts. What are you cultivating your life to
be—a fruitful garden or a poisonous marsh?

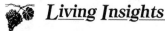 ## *Living Insights*

In the Sermon on the Mount, Jesus tells us how to distinguish
true teachers from false ones. They can be identified in the same
way that trees can—by the fruit they produce (Matt. 7:15–20).
This fruit is harvested for us in Galatians 5:19–23 and placed into
two bushel baskets: the deeds of the flesh and the fruit of the Spirit.

Pick through 2 Peter 2:12–19 and thump the fruit of the teachers
described in those verses. List their character traits.

_____   _____

_____   _____

_____   _____

_____   _____

_____   _____

_____

Now travel down the next aisle over and examine the fruit of
good teachers in 1 Timothy 4:6–5:2. List the character traits that
Paul encourages.

_____   _____

_____   _____

_____   _____

_____   _____

Using Galatians 5:19–23 as your fruit inspector, examine these two bushels of character traits. What might be the result if you were fed by someone with the qualities found in 2 Peter 2:12–19?

_____

_____

_____

What might be the result if you were nourished by someone with the characteristics found in 1 Timothy 4:6–5:2?

_____

_____

_____

Describe the qualities of the teacher who is presently providing you nourishment.

_____

_____

_____

_____

How would you describe the diet of truth you receive from that person?

_____

_____

_____

If you are being deprived of some vital nutrients, how might you supplement your diet?

_____

_____

_____

In the concluding section of today's lesson, we highlighted the fact that *we are to live the truth . . . no matter what.* Take a minute or two to evaluate how well you're doing that in the following areas.

Your Walk with God

- Do you most often
  - ☐ lag behind Him?
  - ☐ run ahead of Him?
  - ☐ keep in step with Him?

- Do you talk with Him
  - ☐ rarely?
  - ☐ occasionally?
  - ☐ regularly?

- When you talk with Him, is the communication
  - ☐ hurried and abrupt?
  - ☐ guarded and defensive?
  - ☐ open and honest?

- When you communicate with Him, do you
  - ☐ do all the talking?
  - ☐ run out of things to say after a few minutes?
  - ☐ have a good balance between talking and listening?

Your Responsiveness to the Counsel of His Word

- Do you turn to His Word
  - ☐ as a last resort?
  - ☐ on occasion?
  - ☐ instinctively?

- Do you
  - ☐ agree with its counsel intellectually but fail to heed it volitionally?
  - ☐ obey partially or slowly?
  - ☐ obey promptly and fully?

The Promptings of Your Heart

- Do you feel your heart prompting you
  - ☐ rarely?
  - ☐ occasionally?
  - ☐ regularly?

- Do you respect the promptings of your heart
  - ☐ rarely?
  - ☐ occasionally?
  - ☐ regularly?
- If you feel a certain intuitive reluctance toward a teacher, do you
  - ☐ ignore that feeling?
  - ☐ continue to be involved until some tangible discrepancy surfaces?
  - ☐ honor that feeling and hold back?

How Closely You Follow the Example of Christ

- Do you follow His example
  - ☐ when it's convenient?
  - ☐ when you're around other Christians, primarily?
  - ☐ the best you can in every circumstance?

Looking over this self-evaluation, do you see any area that jumps out at you as a glaring inconsistency in your life? If so, describe it.

_____

_____

_____

_____

What one thing could you do this week to help improve in that area?

_____

_____

Can you think of any passage of Scripture that could give you guidance to help correct that inconsistency?

_____

_____

Chapter 7

WHICH IS WORST?
WHAT IS BEST?

2 Peter 2:20–3:2

One of the world's best known maxims was penned by the poet laureate of England—Alfred, Lord Tennyson.

> 'Tis better to have loved and lost
> Than never to have loved at all.[1]

That may be so with love and romance, but it's not with knowledge and truth. It's *not* better to have heard the truth and turned from it than never to have known the truth at all. In other words, as Peter will explain, ignorance is better than apostasy.

A Brief Review, Which Answers "Which Is Worse?"

Before we look closely at Peter's explanation of which is worse—turning from or not knowing the truth—let's refresh our memories with a little background information. Peter opens chapter two with a warning about false teachers who secretly traffic in counterfeit truth (2 Peter 2:1). From there, he launches into the most severe denunciation of religious apostates in all of his writings (vv. 1–19). Peter says that though they appear to be resourceful and sincere, they're empty and deceitful. They appear to have answers and hope, but they lack the truth and bring others down. They appear to be communicating reliable information with biblical terms, but they twist the meaning of those terms to misrepresent the truth. They appear to be free and offer freedom, but they are enslaved to sin and lead others into that same bondage.

The Consequence

In verse 13, Peter warned that these apostles of Satan will "suffer wrong as the wages of doing wrong." In verse 20, he amplifies his statement.

---

1. Alfred, Lord Tennyson, "In Memoriam," as quoted in *Masterpieces of Religious Verse*, ed. James Dalton Morrison (New York, N.Y.: Harper and Brothers Publishers, 1948), p. 298.

> For if after they have escaped the defilements of the
> world by the knowledge of the Lord and Savior Jesus
> Christ, they are again entangled in them and are
> overcome, the last state has become worse for them
> than the first.

False teachers know about Jesus Christ intellectually. They use His words, invoke His name, and carry His book. But they do not know Him personally. Theirs is an academic knowledge, not a saving faith.

Knowing God's truth, however, does have some benefits. Peter says that by it even false teachers can escape some of the defilements of the world. But their perverted teaching of grace, which gives license to sin, will eventually ensnare them in worse defilements than the ones they practiced before knowing the truth.

The Question

The plight of false teachers going from bad to worse raises an important question: Is it better to have had at least an intellectual knowledge of God's Word than never to have known it at all? Peter anticipated this and provided an answer, a very surprising one, in verse 21.

> For it would be better for them not to have known
> the way of righteousness, than having known it, to
> turn away from the holy commandment delivered to
> them.

In other words, ignorance is better than defection. To illustrate this, Peter then compared the ways of the false teachers to those of a dog and a hog.

> It has happened to them according to the true prov-
> erb, "A dog returns to its own vomit," and, "A sow,
> after washing, returns to wallowing in the mire."
> (v. 22)

Dogs in Peter's day were regarded with contempt, unlike today's dog which is bathed, groomed, and pampered as a beloved pet. Underneath it all, however, a dog's nature stays the same—a dog is a dog is a dog. And most dogs have the repulsive habit of returning to their own vomit, just as a freshly bathed pig will wallow in mud the first chance it gets.

Similarly, false teachers love to wear clerical collars, dress up in religious robes, and preach behind podiums. But they, too, have the repulsive habit of returning to wallow in defilements more despicable than the ones they reveled in before they knew the truth. For underneath, their nature remains unchanged—they are counterfeit to the core.

Peter is emphatic, ignorance is better than apostasy. And here are three reasons why. First: Those who are ignorant can be taught and won to the Lord, but those who know about Christ but have not believed in Christ are less teachable and not as open. It is much more difficult to unlearn something than it is to learn it correctly the first time.

Second: The ignorant are not as influential as the learned. People who claim to have the truth and teach others can develop quite a following. But it would be better to be ignorant and alone than to be responsible for leading many others astray.

Third: In the final judgment, there will be less punishment for the ignorant than for those who heard the truth but turned away. Certainly everyone who rejects the Lord Jesus will spend eternity in hell. But according to Jesus' parable in Luke 12:41–48, apparently there will be less punishment for those who never knew Him than for those who knew His truth and turned away.

> "And that slave who knew his master's will and did not get ready or act in accord with his will, shall receive many lashes, but the one who did not know it, and committed deeds worthy of a flogging, will receive but few. And from everyone who has been given much shall much be required; and to whom they entrusted much, of him they will ask all the more." (vv. 47–48)

A Statement of Purpose, Which Answers "What Is Best?"

Having dealt with the depraved mind, Peter now addresses those with a "sincere mind," reminding them of why he has written such a strong letter.

Why Peter Wrote

> This is now, beloved, the second letter I am writing to you in which I am stirring up your sincere mind by way of reminder. (2 Peter 3:1)

Peter wrote this letter to stimulate wholesome thinking in people he described as having sincere or "sun judged" minds. "Sun judged" is the definition of the Greek word, *eilikrinēs*, that Peter uses for *sincere*. It refers to the old practice in the apostles' day of holding pottery up to the sun to reveal any cracks the potter had tried to hide by filling them with wax. Peter affirms his readers as being people whom he could lift up to the sun and find no wax, no hidden cracks, no deception.

How Should We Respond?

Sincerity doesn't guarantee alertness, however; so Peter writes to stir them up to remember what they have known already.

> That you should remember the words spoken before-hand by the holy prophets and the commandment of the Lord and Savior spoken by your apostles. (v. 2)

Three sources are mentioned here. They are to remember the words spoken by the holy prophets—that's the Old Testament. They're to remember the words spoken by the Lord Jesus—that's the gospels. And they're to remember the words spoken by the apostles—those are the epistles.

A Practical Response, Which Deals with "So What?"

Now that we have looked at the worst and best responses to God's Word, let's close our time with three differences the Scriptures *should* make in our lives.

First: *Since knowledge brings responsibility, we should put into action what we already know.* Many of us already know far more than we're practicing. And yet we keep right on buying more books, going to more seminars, and signing up for more Bible studies. Remember, though, that knowledge alone tends to puff up our pride, not foster our obedience—the more we learn, the more God expects us to *apply*. And the more obedient we become, the more He will mold us into sincere, sun-judged followers. Instead of seeking more knowledge, do you need to focus on applying what you already know?

Second: *Since responsibility means accountability, we should be able to endure examination.* This is where false teachers fail. If you look close enough, holding what they're saying up to the light of God's Word, you'll see the cracks filled with wax.

Third: *Since accountability is to be expected, we should return often to orthodox truth.* Rather than relying on visions, dreams, and extra-biblical extravaganzas, we need to place our reliance in the orthodox truth of God's Word.

🍇 *Living Insights*   STUDY ONE

Let's dig into 2 Peter 2:20–22 by sinking an inquisitive shovel into the text to unearth some of its deeper truths. For some of these, you may need a good concordance or a Bible with margin notes.

What are some of the interpretive options for who "they" refers to in verse 20? Support each answer with a verse from chapter 2.

1. _____

2. _____

How does the verbal metaphor *entangled* shed light on the nature of the "defilements of the world" in verse 20?

_____

_____

The words "the last state has become worse for them than the first" are an echo of what New Testament passage?

_____

Define "the holy commandment" in verse 21.

_____

_____

"A dog returns to its own vomit" is a quote from which specific Old Testament verse?

_____

Considering that Peter was called to minister to the Jews (Gal. 2:7), why are the images of the dog and pig particularly poignant?

_____

_____

What hope is there for those whose nature, like a dog or a pig, is bent on returning to old habits (see 2 Cor. 5:17 and Eph. 4:17–32)?

_____

_____

🍇 *Living Insights* STUDY TWO

Deliberately choosing to walk down a wrong path is a dangerous means of going astray. But there is another way to get lost in the woods—by simply forgetting which is the right path. Second Peter 2:20–22 addresses those who defiantly chart a sinful course in life. Chapter 3, verses 1–2, speaks to those who merely need a little refresher course in map reading.

Consult a concordance or simply chase down the cross references to the word *remember* in 2 Peter 3:2. Seek out only the verses that tell us what *we* are to remember (skip the ones that talk about God remembering). Then summarize what it is that we are to remember and explain why. Choose half your verses from the Old Testament and half from the New.

Remember
Old Testament Passages

Where: _____

What: _____

Why: _____

_____

Where: _____

What: _____

Why: _____

_____

Where: _____

What: _____

Why: _____

_____

New Testament Passages

Where: _____

What: _____

Why: _____

_____

Where: _____

What: _____

Why: _____

_____

Where: _____

What: _____

Why: _____

_____

Of these, which one do *you* most need to be stirred up to remember?

_____

Why? _____

_____

What could you do that would tie a string around your mental finger to help remember this?

_____

_____

Chapter 8

SKEPTICS AND SINNERS, BEWARE!

2 Peter 3:1–7

Most biblical promises bring us a great deal of comfort and relief. Most. A few, however, leave our stomachs in knots. Like the promise Paul wrote to Timothy. Writing from a Roman dungeon, Paul commends the young pastor for his commitment, and then adds a very unsettling promise.

> But you followed my teaching, conduct, purpose, faith, patience, love, perseverance, persecutions, and sufferings, such as happened to me at Antioch, at Iconium and at Lystra; what persecutions I endured, and out of them all the Lord delivered me! *And indeed, all who desire to live godly in Christ Jesus will be persecuted.* (2 Tim. 3:10–12, emphasis added)

That's a promise. But it's a promise of persecution, not comfort. Paul is not talking about mild disagreements or troubles because of our own wrongdoings; he's talking about blatant mocking and rejection for following Christ.

When was the last time you experienced the fulfillment of that promise? Was it last week? Last month? Perhaps it was last year or when you first became a Christian. Or is it possible you've never been the brunt of someone's deliberate persecution? In case you haven't experienced any overt mocking yet, don't worry, you will. Paul guarantees it, and history confirms it.

A Brief Review of Contrary Forces

Let's take a brief look back at some of the persecutions believers have endured in ages past.

In Old Testament Days

Noah: It took Noah 120 years to build an ark designed by God for a rain no one had ever seen before. And all this work was done among people so corrupt that God was sorry He had made them

(Gen. 6:5–6). Ridicule? Persecution? You bet they mocked that "crazy old fanatic," right up until the ark's door closed and the clouds burst open.

Moses: Consider Moses, who was openly attacked by his own people on several occasions for leading them out of Egypt and into the wilderness (Exod. 17:1–4; Num. 11:1–15). And there was the time when even Miriam and Aaron, Moses' own sister and brother, mockingly questioned his right to be the sole recipient of God's messages (Num. 12:1–2).

David: David went from being favored as King Saul's personal musician to being persecuted as the king's personal enemy. It started with Saul becoming suspicious of David. Then he tried to pin David to the wall with a spear. After missing a second time, the king decided to hurl his whole army at him. For years, David lived like a hunted animal, in caves, always on the move, persecuted by a king gone mad (1 Sam. 16–26).

Elijah: The prophet Elijah squared off with the prophets of Baal on Mount Carmel and proved that Jehovah was the only true God. The people were responsive, but the wicked Queen Jezebel definitely was not. Those were her pet prophets Elijah killed, and she immediately threatened to do the same to him (1 Kings 18:1–19:4).

Nehemiah: When Nehemiah began the work of rebuilding Jerusalem's walls, Tobiah the Ammonite, Sanballat the Horonite, and Geshem the Arab immediately went to work mocking and scoffing the project. But despite their repeated verbal bashings, the wall was built in record time (Neh. 2:19; 4:1–3; 6:15).

In New Testament Times

Over in the gospels, Jesus faced scoffings from scribes, persecutions from Pharisees, and rejection from Roman officials. He even had to endure the humiliation of having his own family treat him as if He were insane (Mark 3:21).

Then there was Stephen, the faithful deacon of the early church who refused to deny the Lord, only to become the first martyr (Acts 6:8–7:60). And don't forget Paul and his missionary companions. Everywhere they traveled they were hated, misunderstood, mocked, maligned, and rejected because of the truth they preached. Paul even named one individual who persecuted him.

> Alexander the coppersmith did me much harm; the
> Lord will repay him according to his deeds. Be on

guard against him yourself, for he vigorously opposed our teaching. (2 Tim. 4:14–15)

Throughout Church History

Space doesn't permit us to name names here, but anyone familiar with history knows that scoffers have hounded Christians down through the centuries. From Wycliffe to Wilberforce,[1] every servant of God who vigorously proclaimed the gospel had their heels dogged by the savage teeth of hatred and persecution. For the early reformers, that persecution became so intense that in order to survive they had to develop some pretty forceful styles of their own. Philip Schaff described Martin Luther in his series *History of the Christian Church*:

> Luther was a man of war. . . . Luther's writings smell of powder; his words are battles; he overwhelms his opponents with a roaring cannonade of argument, eloquence, passion, and abuse.[2]

When you hold the promise of persecution up to the annals of history, you might get the impression that mockers will always have their say and that persecutions will never stop. But Peter has some good news for us. A day is coming when all scoffers will be silenced; all persecutions, stopped.

Strong Reassurance for the Godly

Peter first introduces this good news with some reassuring words for those godly believers currently experiencing persecution.

Remember the Words

> This is now, beloved, the second letter I am writing to you in which I am stirring up your sincere mind by way of reminder, that you should remember the words spoken beforehand by the holy prophets and the commandment of the Lord and Savior spoken by your apostles. (2 Pet. 3:1–2)

1. John Wycliffe (c. 1330–1384) was a brilliant scholar and English reformer who translated the first English version of the Bible from the Latin Vulgate. William Wilberforce (1759–1833), a member of the British Parliament, was converted at twenty-five and later led a movement to abolish the slave trade. For further study concerning persecution throughout church history, see *Foxe's Book of Martyrs* and *Tortured for Christ* by Richard Wurmbrand.

2. Philip Schaff, *Modern Christianity: The German Reformation*, vol. 7 of *History of the Christian Church*, 2d ed., rev. (1910; reprint, Grand Rapids, Mich.: William B. Eerdmans Publishing Co., 1960), p. 194.

When the mocking gets ugly and the flak is heavy, who do you turn to for help? Your friends? Your parents? Certainly these can be good, but they're not the best. The best source of reassurance and encouragement is God Himself through His timeless Word.

Remember Who Spoke Them

When we read the words of the prophets, the Savior, and the apostles, we're reading the veteran words of people who have been at war. When Satan tempted Christ in the wilderness, Jesus replied each time with a salvo from the Scriptures, "It is written" (Matt. 4:4, 7, 10). Outside Scripture, no other writers or words have such power or can offer such reassurance.

Sober Warnings to the Ungodly

In verses 3–7 Peter sets forth some sobering facts regarding the fate of the ungodly. In verses 3–4 he presents something to know about the present. In verses 5–6 there is something to remember from the past. And in verse 7 there is something to count on in the future.

Something to Know about the Present

> Know this first of all, that in the last days mockers will come with their mocking, following after their own lusts, and saying, "Where is the promise of His coming? For ever since the fathers fell asleep, all continues just as it was from the beginning of creation." (vv. 3–4)

In the days in which we live, called here "the last days," Peter assures us there will be mockers. And one of their favorite topics to ridicule will be Christ's return. "According to the laws of nature," they say, "life is simply one continuous line of unbroken existence. And since this existence knows no interruption, the idea of Jesus returning and altering our earthly existence is preposterous." The theory undergirding this view is called *uniformitarianism*, and it is founded on the bedrock of humanistic philosophy. Peter counters this shortsighted skepticism, however, with a brief history lesson from Genesis.

Something to Remember from the Past

> For when they maintain this, it escapes their notice that by the word of God the heavens existed long

ago and the earth was formed out of water and by
water, through which the world at that time was
destroyed, being flooded with water. (vv. 5–6)

The main problem with the theory of uniformitarianism is just
that, it's simply a theory. Not only has it not been proven, but the
Greek phrase, "it escapes their notice," suggests that these same
people deliberately ignore God's hand in creation. They willfully
overlook the fact that God already interrupted time past with a
universal flood. As a consequence, the world, nature, and human-
kind were dramatically altered.

Knowing that God intervened in the past, Peter then points
out a logical reminder about the future.

Something to Count on in the Future

But the present heavens and earth by His word are
being reserved for fire, kept for the day of judgment
and destruction of ungodly men. (v. 7)

Peter's point is simple. If God intervened before, He can do it
again. And He will. Only this time, instead of using water, God
will judge the world with fire.

But the day of the Lord will come like a thief, in
which the heavens will pass away with a roar and
the elements will be destroyed with intense heat,
and the earth and its works will be burned up. (v. 10)

This is the end of the line, the frightening apocalypse that
awaits all mockers who willfully ignore God's truth and persecute
His children.

A Final Reminder about God's Judgment

If you know that something cataclysmic is coming, you prepare
for it, right? At least that's what everybody says. But not everyone
does. Many in California, for example, are still putting off preparing
an earthquake kit to help them survive "the big one." When it hits,
water supplies will be contaminated, electric lines will be down,
gas lines ruptured, homes destroyed, people hurt—everything will
be in chaos, and these people will be totally unprepared.

The question concerning God's future cataclysmic judgment of
the world is not, "Is it coming?" The question is, "Will you be ready

for it *when* it comes?" Are you prepared with an indestructible faith in Jesus Christ? Or will you be swept away like those scoffers who stood outside the ark pounding on the door to get in? God *is* going to intervene again, the scoffing *will* cease, and everyone *will* believe —only for some it will be too late. Are you final-judgment prepared?

🍇 *Living Insights* STUDY ONE

The book of Proverbs pencils an unflattering character sketch of the scoffer. Look up the following verses and shade in the details.

9:7 _____

13:1 _____

14:6 _____

15:12 _____

21:24 _____

24:9 _____

How does the Lord respond to scoffers (Prov. 3:34)?

_____

How should we respond to them?

Psalm 1:1 _____

Proverbs 9:8 _____

Have there been times when you have sat in the seat of scoffers and ridiculed God's truth or the proclaimers of His truth? Briefly describe one of those times.

_____

_____

If so, what change took place in your heart that prevented you from going back to that pretentious seat of judgment?

_____

_____

Like some of the biblical characters mentioned in this lesson, have you been the target of ridicule from the hands of scoffers and skeptics? If so, cite an example.

_____

_____

_____

_____

How did those attacks make you feel?

_____

_____

How did you respond in your mind?

_____

_____

How did you respond in your speech and actions?

_____

_____

_____

How does the Scripture advise you to respond?

Matthew 5:10–12 _____

_____

Matthew 5:44 _____

_____

1 Corinthians 13:4–5 _____

_____

1 Peter 2:21–23 _____

_____

2 Corinthians 6:1–10 (esp. v. 3) _____

_____

Romans 8:31–39 _____

_____

Is there anyone presently mocking your beliefs or your behavior? If so, start praying for that person. At worst, it could improve your attitude; at best, it could change that person.

Chapter 9

THE DAY OF THE LORD

2 Peter 3:8–13

The Christians of Peter's day looked with anxiety toward their future. Not only were apostate scoffers creating doubts and confusion about Christ's return, but these early believers were having to endure some of the most horrible persecutions imaginable. Here is one historian's account of those tragic times.

> In the meantime, the number of Christians being now very large, it happened that Rome was destroyed by fire, while Nero was stationed at Antium. But the opinion of all cast the odium of causing the fire upon the emperor, and he was believed in this way to have sought for the glory of building a new city. And, in fact, Nero could not, by any means he tried, escape from the charge that the fire had been caused by his orders. He, therefore, turned the accusation against the Christians, and the most cruel tortures were accordingly inflicted upon the innocent. Nay, even new kinds of death were invented, so that, being covered in the skins of wild beasts, they perished by being devoured by dogs, while many were crucified, or slain by fire . . . that, when the day came to a close, they should be consumed to serve for light during the night. In this way, cruelty first began to be manifested against the Christians. Afterwards, too, their religion was prohibited by laws which were enacted; and by edicts openly set forth it was proclaimed unlawful to be a Christian.[1]

Outlawed, maligned, tortured, and murdered—the future looked bleak to those first-century Christians. In chapter 3 of Peter's second letter, verses 8–13, the seasoned apostle calmed their fears and strengthened their hope with a close look at God's plan for the future.

---

1. Sulipicius Severus, *Chronicle,* quoted by William Barclay in *The Letters of James and Peter,* rev. ed., The Daily Study Bible Series (Philadelphia, Pa.: Westminster Press, 1976), ¬ 149–50.

Several Facts about the Future, in General

To begin, let's address four general facts or warnings about the future.

First: *While some things are revealed, much still remains a mystery.* One of the marks of an immature Christian is the tendency to read into a text more than it actually states. And no other topic of Scripture receives more overzealous interpretations than prophecy. God has told us a great deal about the future that we can understand. But there are still many biblical passages that remain a mystery. So, be cautious about trying to unravel all of it yourself or about following those who claim they can.

Second: *When searching for answers, continue to leave room for questions.* Also, don't make agreement on future events the basis of fellowship with other believers. Leave room for those who still have questions and for those who have a different perspective than your own.

Third: *Though no one knows all the details, don't hesitate to stand firm on those clearly set forth in Scripture.* As far as the precise chronology of future events is concerned, no one really knows for certain. And as we said before, those are the kinds of issues we shouldn't demand unanimity on in order to be unified in fellowship with other believers. However, many truths about the future are plainly revealed in the Scriptures. For example, God has made it clear that there will be a resurrection from the dead, that Christ will come again to this earth, that everyone will give an account of their lives before God, and that heaven and hell are real. These, like many others, are sure. So just remember, don't be afraid to let what you don't know for sure keep you from standing firm on what you *do* know is certain.

Fourth: *As you stand firm on certain points, be patient with those who do not agree with you.* Perhaps someday the differences between you and another person will be resolved. Perhaps not. Whatever the case, agree to disagree without rejecting the other person.

Specific Truth concerning Earth, in Particular

At the close of our last lesson, Peter assured his readers that the present heavens and earth are "reserved for fire, kept for the day of judgment and destruction of ungodly men" (2 Pet. 3:7). Knowing that this statement would pique the interest of those Christians whose very lives were being destroyed by the ungodly, Peter goes on to describe God's judgment plan in greater detail.

God's Mysterious Timetable

The first specific truth Peter offers concerns God's timing.

> But do not let this one fact escape your notice,
> beloved, that with the Lord one day is as a thousand
> years, and a thousand years as one day. (v. 8; see
> also Ps. 90:4)

What does Peter mean? He's saying that what comprises time on earth in no way impacts God's master plan in heaven. The Lord dwells above and apart from our twenty-four-hour day.

Because of this discrepancy between earth and divine time, scoffers suggest that God hasn't kept His promise to return (see 2 Pet. 3:3–4). But Peter says that we can't use a watch to disprove God's game plan for the future; He may appear to be late in acting, but He's never delayed.

But Peter also knows of one other important facet to God's timing.

Salvation's Patient Plan

What appears as God's mysterious timetable in verse 8 is revealed to be salvation's patient plan in verse 9.

> The Lord is not slow about His promise, as some
> count slowness, but is patient toward you, not wishing
> for any to perish but for all to come to repentance.

The Lord is not slow—He is patient. The Lord is not tardy—He is deliberately waiting. The Lord is not indifferent—He is merciful. He is holding back the events of the end to give as many people as possible an opportunity to believe in His Son. The apostle Paul also wrote about this in 1 Timothy 2,

> God our Savior . . . desires all men to be saved and
> to come to the knowledge of the truth. (vv. 3b–4)

Just imagine, what if the Lord had ended all things just moments before you believed? Or make it personal in another way. Think of some people you know who are not Christians, and put their name in place of the words "any" and "all" in 2 Peter 3:9. Does this help you see that what may seem slow now is, in fact, God's mercy in action? Remember, God is not only patiently waiting for that person and all other non-Christians to believe in Him, He's also waiting for us to share the good news of salvation so that they can believe (see Rom. 10:17)!

It's true that God, in His generous mercy, is waiting patiently for us. But as Peter assures us, even God's patience will come to an end, cutting off abruptly with His final judgment.

> But the day of the Lord will come like a thief, in which the heavens will pass away with a roar and the elements will be destroyed with intense heat, and the earth and its works will be burned up. (2 Pet. 3:10)

Let's answer a few reporters' questions about this awesome "day of the Lord."

When? Jesus uses the analogy in Matthew 24:42–44 that Paul does in 1 Thessalonians 5:2: "like a thief." What does this analogy mean? That no one knows when a thief will strike and, like a thief, the end will come suddenly—unexpectedly . . . surprisingly . . . strategically.

What? Three phrases in verse 10 tell us what will happen. The "heavens will pass away," the "elements will be destroyed," and "the earth and its works will be burned up." In verse 12 Peter adds another detail to this devastating picture:

> The heavens will be destroyed by burning, and the elements will melt with intense heat! (v. 12b)

How? To answer this, let's examine the meaning behind four words in verse 10, "roar," "destroy," and "intense heat." The word *roar* was used to describe the whistling of an arrow through space, the rush of wings, or the crackling of the devouring flames of a forest fire. These will be the sounds of heaven when it passes away. Next, Peter states that the basic four elements of the universe—fire, air, earth, and water—will be destroyed. The word for *destroyed* literally means "dissolved by a violent, consuming heat." It may well be that the atomic power stored within the elements will be released instantaneously, obliterating everything.

Who? The final end of this world will come not because some nervous military ruler "pushes the button" and begins an apocalyptic nuclear war. It is God Himself who will push the button to end this world. He created the heavens and the earth we live in, and He has reserved the sole right to bring both to an end, in His own timing and in His own way.

Our Marching Orders

Typically, whenever prophetic truth is set forth in Scripture, the Lord comes back and says, "Now in light of that, here's how you ought to live." Prophecy is never meant to be an end in itself. The purpose of prophetic truth is not speculation, it's motivation—it is designed to light a fire under our lives and fan the flame of godly living. So what are we to do while waiting for the Day of the Lord to come?

> Since all these things are to be destroyed in this way, what sort of people ought you to be in holy conduct and godliness, looking for and hastening the coming of the day of God. . . . But according to His promise we are looking for new heavens and a new earth, in which righteousness dwells. (vv. 11, 12a, 13)

Our marching orders can be summed up in three commands: *Clean up. Look up. Speak up.* Clean up your life. Look up and expect His coming. Speak up every chance you get because His coming will not be delayed forever. And do what this young medical student determined to do.

> In the spring of 1871, a young man picked up a book and read twenty-one words that had a profound effect on his future. A medical student at the Montreal General Hospital, he was worried about passing the final examination, worried about what to do, where to go, how to build up a practice, how to make a living.
>
> The twenty-one words that this young medical student read in 1871 helped him to become the most famous physician of his generation. He organized the world-famous Johns Hopkins School of Medicine. He became Regius Professor of Medicine at Oxford —the highest honor that can be bestowed upon any medical man in the British Empire. He was knighted by the King of England. When he died, two huge volumes containing 1466 pages were required to tell the story of his life.
>
> His name was Sir William Osler. Here are the twenty-one words that he read in the spring of 1871 —twenty-one words from Thomas Carlyle that helped

him lead a life free from worry: *"Our main business is not to see what lies dimly at a distance, but to do what lies clearly at hand."*[2]

Are you doing the things that lie clearly at hand—cleaning up, looking up, speaking up—or are you too busy arguing over what lies dimly in the future?

For each of us, doing what lies clearly at hand will mean different things. If you're not a Christian, nothing is more important than your eternal destiny. God has provided the way for you to be saved through His Son, Jesus Christ (see 1 Tim. 2:5–6; Rom. 6:23). Are you ready to deal with your need for salvation, which lies clearly at hand?

🍇 *Living Insights*   STUDY ONE

Let's take a few minutes to distill some applications from a couple of Christ's parables about the end times.

First, read the parable of the ten virgins in Matthew 25:1–13. What is the application you derive from that story?

_____

_____

What adjective is used to describe the virgins who entered the wedding feast?

_____

How does your life demonstrate this quality in regard to the coming of Christ?

_____

_____

Now read the next parable in Matthew 25:14–30. What is the application you wring from this passage?

_____

_____

2. Dale Carnegie, *How to Stop Worrying and Start Living*, quoted in *Great Quotes and Illustrations*, comp. George Sweeting (Waco, Tex.: Word Books, 1985), pp. 212–13.

What do the three servants have in common?

_____

What do the first two have in common?

_____

What adjectives does the master use to describe these two servants?

_____

What is their reward? _____

What should we be doing until our Master returns (see Matt. 25:31–40)?

_____

_____

_____

_____

_____

The study of the "end times" is known as *eschatology*. In most evangelical seminaries, it's a course the student body is required to take. But for the rest of the body of Christ, it's a subject most are ignorant of. If you would like to grow in your knowledge of this vital topic, the following recommendations will help.

The first place you will want to start your study is the Olivet Discourse in Matthew 24–25. It is the most detailed teaching by Christ on the subject.

For a succinct theological examination of the end times, see Charles Ryrie's chapter "What Does the Future Hold?" in his book *A Survey of Bible Doctrine*. For an expanded version of his teaching, see the chapter "Things to Come" in his book *Basic Theology*. For a more applicational treatment of the subject, turn to the chapter "The Return of Christ" in Charles Swindoll's *Growing Deep in the Christian Life*. If these have whetted your appetite for a more in-depth study, there are two exhaustive sources we can recommend: J. Dwight Pentecost's *Thy Kingdom Come*; and John F. Walvoord's *The Prophecy Knowledge Handbook*.

The end times have long been the podium of scholarly debate. But the revelation in Scripture about the prophetic scheme of things was given not for our speculation but for our motivation. What three things should we be motivated to do?

Matthew 6:10 _____

Matthew 24:14 _____

2 Peter 3:11 _____

The question Peter poses in today's lesson is a poignant one: "Since all these things are to be destroyed in this way, what sort of people ought you to be in holy conduct and godliness?" Try answering that question as it relates to you personally.

_____

_____

_____

_____

Look up the following Scriptures to see how we should prepare ourselves to meet our coming Lord.

2 Corinthians 11:2; Ephesians 5:27; and Revelation 19:7–8 _____

_____

_____

James 1:27 _____

_____

1 John 2:15–17 _____

_____

Chapter 10

HOW TO LIVE IN TROUBLED TIMES

2 Peter 3:14–18

Whenever Peter's name is mentioned, we don't automatically think of him as a writer of Scripture. Instead, we see a man who was a fisherman, became a leader among the disciples, walked on water, denied the Lord, was later restored to ministry, and became a leader in the early church. But a New Testament writer? No, somehow this important part of Peter's resumé is often overlooked.

Letters may not be the first thing that comes to mind when we think of Peter; but when fears of an uncertain future worry us and when we're needing answers about how to live in troubled times, letters are the first thing we should remember about Peter.

A Few Words about Two Letters

Let's briefly review some of the main thoughts that characterize each of Peter's letters.

Peter's First Letter

Peter first wrote to believers scattered over five different Roman provinces because of government persecution. In chapter 1, verse 1, he calls them "aliens," not only because they were scattered, but also because their faith made them the object of hostility in a pagan culture. So the theme developed in 1 Peter is *hope for the hurting.*

Again and again throughout this first letter, the apostle exhorts his readers to turn their attention away from their persecutors to the person of Jesus Christ. He also offers four suggestions regarding their attitude during times of trial. First, he encourages them to rejoice rather than resent or retaliate (1:6; 4:12–13); second, to submit rather than fight and fume (2:18–25); third, to glorify God, not the pain (4:14–16); and fourth, to remain humble and not become defensive (5:6–7).

His Second Letter

Peter's second letter, though shorter than the first, is much more difficult to understand. Also, it doesn't spend much time emphasizing hope for the hurting. Instead, this letter punches a long index finger against the reader's sternum and soberly warns, "Beware! Be ready! Trouble is upon you!"

Beginning in chapter 1, he warns us against moral corruption. In chapter 2, he urges us to be ready and discerning so that we're not deceived by false teachers. Lastly, in chapter 3, Peter silences scoffers with a reminder of God's past and future judgments.

From the themes alone, one can see that Peter takes on two different roles in his letters. In 1 Peter the emphasis is on helping people. He writes as a shepherd bringing comfort to his persecuted and far-flung flock. In 2 Peter the emphasis is on exposing perilous conditions, and Peter is more like a prophet bringing warnings and predictions. Let's turn to the last chapter in his second letter now, ready to receive some more strong and sober instruction.

Strong Words for Handling Today

As we come to Peter's closing thoughts in verses 14–18, we find that instead of winding down with a few soft platitudes, Peter parts company using four forceful commands.

Be Diligent

> Therefore, beloved, since you look for these things, be diligent to be found by Him in peace, spotless and blameless. (v. 14)

Do your best, Peter says, to keep from drifting into doubt while you wait for God's plans to be fulfilled. Be diligent to be at peace in Him and to keep your character without fault and beyond reproach.

Be Confident

> And regard the patience of our Lord to be salvation; just as also our beloved brother Paul, according to the wisdom given him, wrote to you, as also in all his letters, speaking in them of these things, in which are some things hard to understand, which the un-taught and unstable distort, as they do also the rest of the Scriptures, to their own destruction.[1] (vv. 15–16)

1. Nowhere else in the New Testament will you find a passage like this, where one writer of Scripture refers to another. Contained in this reference are three helpful insights about the apostle Paul. First, Peter reveals that Paul's letters had already begun to be distributed

Scoffers say that the Lord's delay in returning means that He isn't coming at all. But Peter encourages us to be confident as he reaffirms the truth that God's delay is really an expression of His compassion and mercy—that he is patiently giving the lost more opportunities to believe.

Also, between the lines of verses 15–16 is the same warning Peter has sounded since we began chapter 2—beware of religious phonies. Look at the word *distort* in verse 16. The Greek root is actually a very graphic term; the noun form refers to an instrument of torture, while the verb can refer to the actual twisting and dislocating of limbs on the rack. False teachers love to twist the truth until they have successfully dislocated the biblical meaning attached to it.

So before you jump on a bandwagon to follow someone, take a good look at what's being taught. Filter what you hear through the Scriptures. Don't allow someone's style or charisma to lure you into accepting anything as truth until you have compared what they say to what the Scriptures teach.

In light of the twisting that counterfeit communicators do to the Word of God, what, then, are the earmarks of reliable Bible study? One of the most insightful pieces ever written on this subject was penned by Professor Bernard Ramm.

> I feel that I have experienced a good session of Bible study:
> —when I felt the teacher took me right into the text and not around it.
> —when I felt we interacted with the text itself and not with the party line beliefs of the teacher.
> —when I felt that I had a better understanding of the text than when I came into the session.
> —when I felt that the time was basically spent in meanings and not in a miscellany of religious platitudes.

---

among the churches (v. 16). Second, Paul's letters are regarded as Scripture, not just helpful correspondence. Peter ends verse 16 by saying that some twist Paul's teachings the same "as they do also the rest of the Scriptures." The word *Scriptures* used here in Greek is *graphē*, the same word Paul uses in 2 Timothy 3:16, "All Scripture is inspired by God and profitable . . ." Third, Peter tells us that some of what Paul wrote is hard to understand. The good news about difficult passages is that they challenge us to think and dig harder in the Scriptures. But the bad news is that false teachers have an easier time distorting difficult passages to suit their own false doctrines.

—and, when I have felt challenged, comforted, encouraged, and practically instructed.[2]

Be On Guard

Peter's third command, found in verse 17, is expressed using an actual military term.

> You therefore, beloved, knowing this beforehand, be on your guard lest, being carried away by the error of unprincipled men, you fall from your own steadfastness.

Peter is forewarning us to constantly guard against being taken captive by the lies of counterfeit communicators. We will lose our steadfastness, our solid foundation in the truth, if we believe what others say without first checking their biblical credentials.

These commands of Peter's are for everyone in every generation. There will never be a time when we can drop our guard against false teachers. We must always be on the alert . . . keep discerning . . . keep filtering. Why? So we will grow.

Grow

> But grow in the grace and knowledge of our Lord and Savior Jesus Christ. To Him be the glory, both now and to the day of eternity. Amen. (v. 18)

Peter also talked about growing in his first letter:

> Like newborn babes, long for the pure milk of the word, that by it you may grow in respect to salvation. (1 Pet. 2:2)

Back in 2 Peter 3:18, Peter follows his exhortation with two guidelines for growing. First, *grow in grace;* second, *grow in knowledge.* The trick is keeping these two in balance. For example, grace will keep you tolerant and loving, while knowledge will keep you strong. Grace will make you compassionate, while knowledge will make you discerning. Grace will help you smile, knowledge will help you think. Grace will result in vulnerability, knowledge will result in stability.

To monitor your balance, ask yourself these questions: Am I keeping grace and knowledge in balance? Am I growing spiritually? Have I come to the place where some of the things that once threw

2. Bernard Ramm, "But It Isn't Bible Study," *Eternity* magazine, February 1960, p. 45.

me, no longer do? Am I stable where I once was not? Can I handle things that I once could not?

Peter's letters are a timeless reminder of a man who grew. He grew from being a headstrong Galilean to a humble apostle, from a simple fisherman to a great fisher of men.

Peter can help you grow too—just remember the next time you're facing some troubled waters, there's a letter with your name on it waiting for you from a retired Galilean fisherman.

Living Insights

Remember how exciting it was to lean against the kitchen wall and have Mom or Dad measure how tall you were? As children, we yearned to grow up and have somebody mark our progress along the way. But when we finally reached that zenith called adulthood, many of us made the mistake of thinking that all our growing years were over.

In today's lesson, Peter counters this mistaken belief with his earnest entreaty to "*grow* in the grace and knowledge of our Lord and Savior Jesus Christ" (2 Pet. 3:18, emphasis added). What kind of progress are you making in this area? Why not use the following questions to mark the rate of your spiritual growth.

Is your life reflecting the grace of Christ? In what specific ways?

_____

_____

_____

In what ways do you know the Lord better this year than last?

_____

_____

_____

How has the grace and knowledge of Christ impacted your life practically?

_____

_____

_____

83

What are some areas you feel the need to grow in?

_____

_____

_____

Take these areas before God right now. Don't put it off, for as
J. I. Packer reminds us,

> The New Testament makes plain that this life, in
> which bodies grow and wear out while characters get
> fixed, is an antechamber, dressing-room and moral
> gymnasium where, whether we know it or not, we
> all in fact prepare ourselves for a future life which
> will correspond for each of us to what we have chosen
> to be, and will have in it more of joy for some and
> distress for others than this world ever knows.[3]

 ## *Living Insights* STUDY TWO

As we've seen in our study of Peter's second epistle, the size of
a letter has little to do with the simplicity of its contents. Often
surprising—and sometimes strange—the little epistle of 2 Peter
nevertheless has a wealth of treasure for those who are diligent
enough to mine it. What are some treasures you have unearthed
from our ten studies together?

1. A Letter That Rattles Our Cage _____

_____

_____

2. To Be Useful and Fruitful, Here's How _____

_____

_____

3. J. I. Packer, *God Has Spoken* (1979; reprint, Grand Rapids, Mich.: Baker Book House,
1988), p. 10.

3. Be Sure of Your Source _____

_____

_____

4. An Exposé of Counterfeit Communicators _____

_____

_____

5. The God of Wrath and Rescue _____

_____

_____

6. Disobedience Gone to Seed _____

_____

_____

7. Which Is Worse? What Is Best? _____

_____

_____

8. Skeptics and Sinners, Beware! _____

_____

_____

9. The Day of the Lord _____

_____

_____

10. How to Live in Troubled Times _____

_____

_____

BOOKS FOR
PROBING FURTHER

Are you more finicky about your physical diet than you are your spiritual diet? If so, 2 Peter has this to say:

Beware! There are no warning labels on pulpits!

Just because somebody wears a "Christian" label doesn't guarantee that the truth is being dished out. We've got to learn to be very picky eaters when it comes to our spiritual nourishment.

Why? Because, unlike America's health industry, the religious realm has no spiritual surgeon general to advise us which teachings are bad for our health. There's no law requiring false teachers to list the basic ingredients behind their teachings to reveal what they're really peddling. But there is 2 Peter. And on behalf of the Great Physician, Peter has issued a clear warning that some religious teachings contain dangerously high levels of counterfeit truth.

Are you in the high-risk group for being deceived spiritually? According to John Sire, many of us are.

> . . . 40 per cent of the American general public indicated they hold the Bible as the primary basis for their religious beliefs. Moreover, "only 23 per cent of the American public categorically deny that the Bible is God's Word while 42 per cent accept it as inerrant. . . ." The Gallup Poll also reveals an appalling ignorance of the Bible among the American populace. This combination of a low degree of knowledge and a high degree of respect for Scripture paves the way for unscrupulous religious teachers to co-opt the Scripture for their own use, claiming scriptural authority for essentially unscriptural ideas.[1]

The books listed here are recommended reading only and, with the exception of works by Charles R. Swindoll, are not available through Insight for Living. If you wish to obtain some of these suggested readings, please contact your local Christian bookstore.

1. James W. Sire, *Scripture Twisting* (Downers Grove, Ill.: InterVarsity Press, 1980), p. 165, regarding a Gallup poll taken for *Christianity Today* and reported in their 21 March 1980 issue, page 21.

If you want to improve your spiritual health and reduce the risk of being deceived, we recommend the following books to supplement your intake of the Word of God.

Boa, Kenneth. *Cults, World Religions and the Occult.* Wheaton, Ill.: SP Publications, Victor Books, 1990. Not only does this book explain the distinctive teachings of numerous religious movements, but it also counsels Christians on how to respond to these spiritual counterfeits with biblical truth and compassion. An excellent resource for learning how to deal with the false teachers of our day.

Friesen, Garry, and J. Robin Maxson. *Decision Making and the Will of God.* Portland, Oreg.: Multnomah Press, 1980. All believers struggle with knowing how to discern the will of God. And many are relying on everything from stoplights to stars to give them God's guidance. But authors Friesen and Maxson offer a better alternative, one that is not only carefully supported with Scripture but also presented in a logical and practical way.

Pentecost, J. Dwight. *Things to Come.* 1958. Reprint. Grand Rapids, Mich.: Zondervan Publishing House, 1964. "Know this first of all, that in the last days . . ." (2 Pet. 3:3). How thorough is your knowledge concerning what Christ and His apostles have revealed about the last days? Did Peter's description that likens them to a "thief in the night" (v. 10) surprise you? If you would like to learn more about and become better prepared for this promised time, this book would be an excellent place to start.

Ryrie, Charles C. *Basic Theology.* Wheaton, Ill.: SP Publications, Victor Books, 1986. We cannot discern error unless we know the truth, so it is crucial that we have a thorough understanding of the foundations of our faith. In this book, Ryrie provides us with just that—a systematic overview of Christianity's basic doctrines, all supported by a myriad of Scripture references.

Sire, James W. *Scripture Twisting.* Downers Grove, Ill.: InterVarsity Press, 1980. Sire has painstakingly isolated twenty separate kinds of reading errors that cultists characteristically make as they interpret the Bible. In doing so, he not only helps us carry out Peter's command to "be on your guard" so that we aren't "carried away by the error of unprincipled men" (2 Pet. 3:17), but he also encourages us to become better readers of Scripture ourselves.

Stott, John R. W. *Basic Christianity.* 2d ed. 1971. Reprint. Grand Rapids, Mich.: William B. Eerdmans Publishing Co., 1989. This book focuses on the identity and work of Jesus Christ, challenges us to acknowledge our need for Him, and encourages us to respond to Him with wholehearted commitment. It should be required reading for all Christians!

Swindoll, Charles R. *The Grace Awakening.* Dallas, Tex.: Word Publishing, 1990. In what may be his most profound book yet, Chuck Swindoll leads us beyond the frustration and guilt of trying to please others and to the freedom and truth of the grace of God.

————. *Growing Deep in the Christian Life.* Portland, Oreg.: Multnomah Press, 1986. Chuck Swindoll walks you through the basic doctrines of the Christian faith, giving a panoramic overview of the best riches in our biblical heritage. Written in his characteristically warm, clear style, this book takes the stuffiness out of doctrine and makes it come alive.

Wiersbe, Warren W. *Be Alert.* Wheaton, Ill.: SP Publications, Victor Books, 1984. Clear, approachable, and highly readable, this commentary will be helpful to anyone who wishes to study the difficult book of 2 Peter in more detail. Wiersbe also includes studies of 2 and 3 John as well as Jude, and in doing so, provides a well-rounded picture of the Christian's need to be alert to false doctrines and teachers.

Ordering Information

This Bible study guide was designed to be used independently or in conjunction with the broadcast of Chuck Swindoll's taped messages on the topic listed below. If you would like to order cassette tapes or further copies of this study guide, please see the information given below and the Order Form provided on the last page of this guide.

Cassette Tapes and Study Guide

CONQUERING THROUGH CONFLICT

It is a brief book, containing only sixty-one verses, yet 2 Peter contains some of the most intense warnings found in the New Testament—warnings about moral corruption, doctrinal compromise, and false prophecy. But don't be intimidated. Second Peter is a power-packed letter that can protect us from being hoodwinked by false teachers and corrupt leaders who sometimes infiltrate the local church.

Alongside the severe warnings, we also find faith-building encouragement in this epistle. Peter avowed with conviction, "We did not follow cleverly devised fables . . . but we were eyewitnesses of His majesty." Despite destructive conflicts within the church, we are assured that, through the unconquerable integrity of God's Word, we can emerge triumphant in the end.

			Calif.*	U.S.	B.C.*	Canada*
CTC	SG	Study Guide	$ 4.20	$ 3.95	$ 5.08	$ 5.08
CTC	CS	Cassette series, includes album cover	31.34	29.50	42.38	40.13
CTC	1–5	Individual cassettes, include messages A and B	5.31	5.00	7.18	6.79

*These prices already include the following charges: for delivery in **California**, 6¼% sales tax; Canada, 7% postage and handling; **British Columbia**, 6% British Columbia sales tax (on tapes only) and 7% postage and handling. The prices are subject to change without notice.

CTC 1-A: *A Letter That Rattles Our Cage*—Survey of 2 Peter
   B: *To Be Useful and Fruitful, Here's How*—2 Peter 1:1–11
CTC 2-A: *Be Sure of Your Source*—2 Peter 1:12–21
   B: *An Exposé of Counterfeit Communicators*—2 Peter 2:1–3

How to Order by Mail

Simply mark on the order form whether you want the series or individual tapes. Mail the form with your payment to the appropriate address listed below. We will process your order as promptly as we can.

United States: Mail your order to the Sales Department at Insight for Living, Post Office Box 4444, Fullerton, California 92634. If you wish your order to be shipped first-class for faster delivery, add 10 percent of the total order amount. Otherwise, please allow four to six weeks for delivery by fourth-class mail. We accept personal checks, money orders, Visa, or MasterCard in payment for materials. Unfortunately, we are unable to offer invoicing or COD orders.

Canada: Mail your order to Insight for Living Ministries, Post Office Box 2510, Vancouver, British Columbia V6B 3W7. Allow approximately four weeks for delivery. We accept personal checks, money orders, Visa, or MasterCard in payment for materials. Unfortunately, we are unable to offer invoicing or COD orders.

Australia, New Zealand, or Papua New Guinea: Mail your order to Insight for Living, Inc., GPO Box 2823 EE, Melbourne, Victoria 3001, Australia. Please allow six to ten weeks for delivery by surface mail. If you would like your order sent airmail, the delivery time may be reduced. Using the United States price as a base, add postage costs—surface or airmail—to the amount of your order. Please use the chart that follows to determine correct postage. Due to fluctuating currency rates, we can accept only personal checks made payable in U.S. funds, international money orders, Visa, or MasterCard in payment for materials.

Overseas: Other overseas residents should mail their orders to our United States office. Please allow six to ten weeks for delivery by surface mail. If you would like your order sent airmail, the delivery time may be reduced. Using the United States price as a base, add postage costs—surface or airmail—to the amount of your order. Please use the chart that follows to determine correct postage. Due to fluctuating currency rates, we can accept only personal checks made payable in U.S. funds, international money orders, Visa, or MasterCard in payment for materials.

Type of Postage	Postage Cost
Surface	10% of total order
Airmail	25% of total order

For Faster Service, Order by Telephone or FAX

For Visa or MasterCard orders, you are welcome to use one of our toll-free numbers between the hours of 8:00 A.M. and 4:30 P.M., Pacific time, Monday through Friday, or our FAX numbers. The numbers to use from anywhere in the United States are **1-800-772-8888** or FAX (714) 773-0932. To order from Canada, call our Vancouver office using **1-800-663-7639** or FAX (604) 596-2975. Vancouver residents, call (604) 596-2910. Australian residents should phone (03) 872-4606. From overseas, call our Sales Department at (714) 870-9161 in the United States.

Our Guarantee

Our cassettes are guaranteed for ninety days against faulty performance or breakage due to a defect in the tape. For best results, please be sure your tape recorder is in good operating condition and is cleaned regularly.

Note: To cover processing and handling, there is a $10 fee for *any* returned check.

Order Form

CTC CS represents the entire *Conquering through Conflict* series in a special album cover, while CTC 1–5 are the individual tapes included in the series. CTC SG represents this study guide, should you desire to order further copies.

Item	Unit Price Calif.*	U.S.	B.C.*	Canada*	Quantity	Amount
CTC CS	$31.34	$29.50	$42.38	$40.13		$
CTC 1	5.31	5.00	7.18	6.79		
CTC 2	5.31	5.00	7.18	6.79		
CTC 3	5.31	5.00	7.18	6.79		
CTC 4	5.31	5.00	7.18	6.79		
CTC 5	5.31	5.00	7.18	6.79		
CTC SG	4.20	3.95	5.08	5.08		
					Subtotal	
					Overseas Residents *Pay U.S. price plus 10% surface postage or 25% airmail. Also, see "How to Order by Mail."*	
					U.S. First-Class Shipping *For faster delivery, add 10% for postage and handling.*	
					Gift to Insight for Living *Tax-deductible in the United States and Canada.*	
					Total Amount Due *Please do not send cash.*	$

If there is a balance: ☐ apply it as a donation ☐ please refund
*These prices already include applicable taxes and shipping costs.

Payment by: ☐ Check or money order made payable to Insight for Living or

☐ Credit card (circle one): Visa MasterCard Number _____

Expiration Date _____ Signature _____
We cannot process your credit card purchase without your signature.

Name _____

Address _____

City _____ State/Province _____

Zip/Postal Code _____ Country _____

Telephone ( ) _____ Radio Station ___ ___ ___ ___
If questions arise concerning your order, we may need to contact you.

Mail this order form to the Sales Department at one of these addresses:
Insight for Living, Post Office Box 4444, Fullerton, CA 92634
Insight for Living Ministries, Post Office Box 2510, Vancouver, BC, Canada V6B 3W7
Insight for Living, Inc., GPO Box 2823 EE, Melbourne, VIC 3001, Australia

Order Form

CTC CS represents the entire *Conquering through Conflict* series in a special album cover, while CTC 1–5 are the individual tapes included in the series. CTC SG represents this study guide, should you desire to order further copies.

Item	Calif.*	Unit Price U.S.	B.C.*	Canada*	Quantity	Amount
CTC CS	$31.34	$29.50	$42.38	$40.13		$
CTC 1	5.31	5.00	7.18	6.79		
CTC 2	5.31	5.00	7.18	6.79		
CTC 3	5.31	5.00	7.18	6.79		
CTC 4	5.31	5.00	7.18	6.79		
CTC 5	5.31	5.00	7.18	6.79		
CTC SG	4.20	3.95	5.08	5.08		
					Subtotal	
		Overseas Residents *Pay U.S. price plus 10% surface postage or 25% airmail. Also, see "How to Order by Mail."*				
		U.S. First-Class Shipping *For faster delivery, add 10% for postage and handling.*				
		Gift to Insight for Living *Tax-deductible in the United States and Canada.*				
		Total Amount Due *Please do not send cash.*				$

If there is a balance: ☐ apply it as a donation ☐ please refund
*These prices already include applicable taxes and shipping costs.

Payment by: ☐ Check or money order made payable to Insight for Living or

☐ Credit card (circle one): Visa   MasterCard   Number _____

Expiration Date _____   Signature _____
We cannot process your credit card purchase without your signature.

Name _____

Address _____

City _____ State/Province _____

Zip/Postal Code _____ Country _____

Telephone ( ) _____ Radio Station ____ ____ ____ ____
If questions arise concerning your order, we may need to contact you.

Mail this order form to the Sales Department at one of these addresses:
Insight for Living, Post Office Box 4444, Fullerton, CA 92634
Insight for Living Ministries, Post Office Box 2510, Vancouver, BC, Canada V6B 3W7
Insight for Living, Inc., GPO Box 2823 EE, Melbourne, VIC 3001, Australia

Order Form

CTC CS represents the entire *Conquering through Conflict* series in a special album cover, while CTC 1–5 are the individual tapes included in the series. CTC SG represents this study guide, should you desire to order further copies.

Item	Calif.*	Unit Price U.S.	B.C.*	Canada*	Quantity	Amount
CTC CS	$31.34	$29.50	$42.38	$40.13		$
CTC 1	5.31	5.00	7.18	6.79		
CTC 2	5.31	5.00	7.18	6.79		
CTC 3	5.31	5.00	7.18	6.79		
CTC 4	5.31	5.00	7.18	6.79		
CTC 5	5.31	5.00	7.18	6.79		
CTC SG	4.20	3.95	5.08	5.08		
					Subtotal	
					Overseas Residents Pay U.S. price plus 10% surface postage or 25% airmail. Also, see "How to Order by Mail."	
					U.S. First-Class Shipping For faster delivery, add 10% for postage and handling.	
					Gift to Insight for Living Tax-deductible in the United States and Canada.	
					Total Amount Due Please do not send cash.	$

If there is a balance: ☐ apply it as a donation ☐ please refund
*These prices already include applicable taxes and shipping costs.

Payment by: ☐ Check or money order made payable to Insight for Living or

☐ Credit card (circle one): Visa   MasterCard   Number _____

Expiration Date _____ Signature _____
We cannot process your credit card purchase without your signature.

Name _____

Address _____

City _____ State/Province _____

Zip/Postal Code _____ Country _____

Telephone ( )_____ Radio Station ___ ___ ___ ___
If questions arise concerning your order, we may need to contact you.

Mail this order form to the Sales Department at one of these addresses:
Insight for Living, Post Office Box 4444, Fullerton, CA 92634
Insight for Living Ministries, Post Office Box 2510, Vancouver, BC, Canada V6B 3W7
Insight for Living, Inc., GPO Box 2823 EE, Melbourne, VIC 3001, Australia